Running
Beyond
Limits

Andrew Murray

First published 2011 by Mountain Media Productions Ltd

Mountain Media Productions Ltd
Old Glen Road
Newtonmore
Inverness-shire PH20 1EB

www.mountain-media.co.uk

Text by Andrew Murray. Foreword by Sir Ranulph Fiennes

Design and layout by Gregor McNeish for Mountain Media Productions Ltd

Set in 11.5pt Aldine Light

Printed by EuroPrint

ISBN-13: 978-0-9562957-2-9

Running Beyond **Limits**

The adventures of an
Ultra Marathon Runner...

Andrew Murray

Training on the south Glen Shiel Ridge. Photo – Donnie Campbell

On the road in far north Scotland. Photo – Richard Else

Contents

A well earned break. Photo – Rieka Goodall

Acknowledgements

I have been blessed with a wonderful family. My gorgeous wife Jennie has always supported me, and even joined me on several runs. Mum and dad encourage me to see "a bit of the world" and my siblings Susie and Iain kept me sane and kept the van on the snowy road during *Scotland2Sahara*.

Richard, Carrie, Meg, Paul and Dom from Triple Echo Productions produced a fantastic record of *Scotland2Sahara* for television, and their generosity, including taking command of the campervan briefly during the trip, was legendary. I'm indebted to Cameron McNeish and Richard Else from Mountain Media for suggesting I write a book, and then editing it so expertly. Gregor McNeish has done a first class job with the graphic design and further editing. Many thanks to Richard Else, Triple Echo, Mike King, RacingThePlanet, Sandbaggers, Likeys, Rieka Goodall, Alan Silcock, Mark Hawker, Toby Wells, Donnie Campbell and my family for contributing images for this book. Thanks to race directors of all the races mentioned for sharing their wisdom and tales with me. Massive thanks to one of the world's greatest adventurers Sir Ran Fiennes for his kind foreword.

There are literally hundreds of friends I would like to thank, including training partners Donnie Campbell and Joe Symonds, and keen supporters of my runs Dave Scott, Jenna Anians, Soph Morrison, Terry Bishop, Toby Wells, Chris Todd, Mike Adams, Rab MacDonald, Mike and Julie Rennie, Ian Reilly, Alan Gillam, Graham Lind, Elise Ross, Duncan Goodall, the Stirling Murdochs, Fi Mitchell, Mark Beaumont, Paul Bateson and Scott Morrison. All these friends, and many others know how much they helped and how much they mean to me, and have contributed immeasurably to the successful fundraising for the Yamaa Trust along with the trust's fundraiser Karen Mathie. Thanks to the over 1200 people who joined me for a run during *S2S* and all those who made this possible, and to numerous competitors and race staff and directors who have over the years lent me kit, sorted my feet, given me advice, and made the miles go faster.

My sponsors have shown a belief and an unconditional faith in me. My principal sponsors Sandbaggers, Tribesports.com, Vivergo Fuels, thinkPR and UK Gear have offered huge support, and I'm also incredibly grateful to Ron Hill, Team Axarsport, GAP, Essemont Marquees, Exceed, Kahtoola, Sports Kilt, Formthotics, Patterson Medical, Injinji, NiteLite, OMM, Garmin, Webasto, Gerber Campervans, Signage, Delimann, North Pole Marathon, Mainetti, Elete Electrolytes and Desert Majesty for their much valued major sponsorship.

Thanks to all who have sent messages of support which have kept me running through tough times and broken feet. I've appreciated each of these, and the generosity of everyone who has donated to the Yamaa Trust. Together we are making a difference in Mongolia.

Thanks to William Tan, the first and only man to do a wheelchair marathon at the North Pole. He showed me that with preparation, training and self belief hard things become easier.

Andrew Murray, *July 2011*

Hitting the Moroccan highway. Photo – Toby Wells

Foreword
Sir Ranulph Fiennes

Arduous running delivers excitement and experience. It challenges and rewards in equal measure. I have for many years enjoyed long distance running.

Past experiences, including running seven marathons in seven days on seven continents, confirm that to combine running and adventure requires meticulous planning, determination and flexibility as well as fitness.

Opportunities to run in remote and beautiful locations are increasing rapidly. Already international running events are organised from the North Pole, to Outer Mongolia, Mount Everest base camp, to the harsh interior of the Antarctic. Having participated in the North Pole marathon, the memories of the perserverance and character of the participants, as well as the spectacular surrounds remain with me.

For many, running has become a major pursuit. Some select a path less travelled, pushing limits and boundaries. For something to be a challenge there must be an element of risk, or chance of failure.

Dr Andrew Murray has competed successfully in some of the world's most extreme races, and has worked as a doctor at these events, which gives him a unique perspective. I followed with great interest his record breaking *Scotland2Sahara*, in which he ran 2659 miles in 78 days from the north of Scotland deep into the Sahara desert battling through varied topography and a harsh European winter.

This fascinating book not only features the author's perspective on the arduous challenges and races he has completed, but offers insight into the preparation that is required for these events, and features interviews with inspiring and interesting characters.

This book will inspire many to reach for, and achieve their own targets. Andrew Murray describes himself as "an ordinary individual", but you will see that his challenges are far from ordinary and I am sure you will enjoy this book and its excellent photographs.

Ranulph Fiennes, *May 2011*

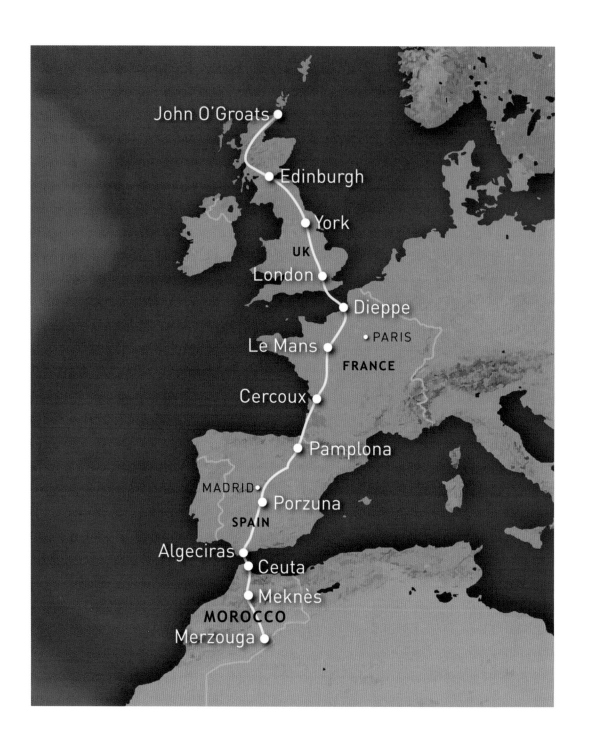

Introduction

"You must be mad…"

"Why," "you must be mad," "is that safe," and "why don't you go and lie on a beach like normal people" are common reactions I've heard before embarking upon the runs described. However responses like "cool," and "is there room for one more" are just as frequent.

Having been privileged enough to see some of the most extraordinary places on earth, and having met numerous amazing people both through running myself, and in my role as an expedition doctor at events, I felt it right to share these experiences. For me there is often an element of competition, but there are far faster and stronger runners out there than I. Running is my way of exploring the world.

Running from the north of Scotland to the Sahara desert, through the arctic in winter, the humid jungle of Indonesia, the mighty Himalaya, in Genghis Khan's hoof prints in Outer Mongolia and many other races has brought massive challenges, but also rewards in far greater measure. The phenomenal views, cultural interaction and cameraderie have far outstripped the pain during such ventures.

This book describes these races and challenges, and meets some of the colourful characters involved. It also provides insight into some of the medical aspects of expeditions and running. I hope you enjoy it.

Andrew

CHAPTER 1

The Planning

"All it takes, is all you've got."

MARK DAVIS

"There is a severe weather warning for North Scotland," announced the radio as the roof of our guesthouse threatened to lift off. John O'Groats on the 8th of November 2010 was not a place for sun worshippers, or anyone else for that matter. A thousand and one thoughts went through my mind as I left the warmth and comfort of our overnight digs and made my way to the starting line. It was bitterly cold. The hot sands of the Sahara seemed like a million miles away as my friends Dave Scott and Rab McDonald, my Mum, and the BBC camera crew gathered round to give me a countdown. Pausing to avoid the waves crashing over the harbour wall I was off, with 2659 miles separating me from my final destination in Morocco.

Preparation for *Scotland2Sahara* had been extensive, or so I had thought. The inspiration for the run had come when I was running the Gobi Challenge in Mongolia. While on the crest of a transient 'runner's high,' I pondered how long it would take to run from Scotland to Mongolia. Dismissing this as ridiculous, I thought jogging to the Sahara might be much more sensible. I was fortunate enough to help with and witness the truly awesome work the Yamaa Trust was doing to ameliorate poverty in the Gobi Desert during that trip, and the hospitality and struggles of the Mongolian people had left a lasting impression. Seven months later in March 2010, I recalled this grand plan while struggling through a blizzard on the Eildon Hills in Scotland.

Training on the south Glen Shiel Ridge. Photo – Donnie Campbell

"Jennie, what do you think of me running to Morocco," I asked. Jennie looked less pleased than when I'd asked her to marry me two months earlier. Her eyes rolled. This was the second time I'd mentioned it and despite my huge grin she realised I was serious.

"When?"

"Well, there is a three month gap between that Indonesia trip, and our wedding. It would make wedding planning way more difficult but it would work."

She took a few minutes to think.

"As long as you're back in plenty time for the wedding," she said eventually.

Game on, I thought. This could be a brilliant year. Getting married and three months running. Amazing.

Mum was less keen than Jennie. "Of all your far-fetched ideas, this is the most ridiculous," she said.

"Ridiculous and ludicrous, I'm out," blasted Duncan Bannatyne of Dragon's Den from the television, with perfect timing.

Mum quickly came round to the master plan following my protestations that it wouldn't be too bad and that she might like to come out for a visit, and the enthusiasm of Dave Scott, a close friend and an experienced expedition organiser and kit supplier, helped get the ball rolling. Dave even looked jealous, and having heard all about his run in the Great Victorian desert I could tell he would be a fantastic mine of information and tips.

Joe Symonds, whose father Hugh had completed an epic 94 day run over all the 3000 foot mountain in Britain and Ireland, and running between them, loved the concept. "You should definitely use your campervan and have folk come along and support you, it helped Dad loads," he suggested. Mark Cooper, who was about to run from Amsterdam to Barcelona suggested it must be some sort of record and gave me contacts that had helped him with his expedition.

Training as usual consisted of playing plenty football, tennis, and squash, while running ever increasing distances. Licking my wounds following a battering at tennis, (I have minimal skills at tennis despite my name!), I tuned into BBC Scotland's Adventure Show. It was just at the point that I had started looking for fundraising ideas, as raising as much money as possible for the Yamaa Trust was going to be a priority for me. Publicising the run on television seemed like a golden opportunity, so I rang the show's executive producer, Richard Else of Triple Echo Productions who immediately loved the idea of following *Scotland2Sahara*.

"That is such a simple concept. People will really get it," he enthused. "One man running from John O'Groats to the Sahara. That will make a brilliant documentary."

With an hour-long television documentary agreed it was time to get into serious organisation. Over the summer things took shape. With my family's backing, I decided to cover the costs of the expedition myself, and donate all corporate and other money to the Yamaa Trust. The response was phenomenal, with the result that it now felt as though I was part of a team attempting *Scotland2Sahara*. Kate, Karen, Jenna, and Team Tribesport would set up a website, Facebook and Twitter accounts, which would keep friends and family updated and involved. I was convinced that the encouragement received from these sources would provide the motivation while I was pushing out 30-odd miles each day. Dave and the Sandbaggers team helped sort all the equipment that would be required to run and camp in the hills, snow and desert, with a motley collection of crampons, sand gaiters, and sleeping bags gathered together in piles in the spare room.

Virtually all my friends wanted to run a section with me, but I realised that setting this up ad hoc could be a nightmare logistically. However I loved the fact that people wished to support me in this way, and they would be getting themselves fit at the same time. As a GP, one of my passions is emphasising the benefits of exercise and activity. The health gain produced by increasing the amount of activity or exercise each person does is astonishing. Statistics from 2005 show that 8.2 billion pounds could be saved by British taxpayers each year if the nation became more active. Amazingly, the potential benefit gained if everyone did an adequate amount of exercise would exceed the benefit if every smoker in the UK stopped. I found these figures mind blowing.

This was a great opportunity, if I could encourage friends, family and even people I had never met to do more activity, *Scotland2Sahara* could really make a difference, and improve the health of individuals and the nation. A call from the Scottish Government's Active Nation team was hugely encouraging. It was a great honour to give a talk on 'The Benefits of Exercise, and Challenging Yourself to reach Personal Targets,' to the Active Nation team, and a bonus to receive the backing of Scotland's First Minister Alex Salmond, who recognised the merits of emphasising this topic and wished me "all the best as you set off on your exciting journey."

Setting up opportunities for others to become involved was a must. We would set up events on the tremendously scenic West Highland Way, another in the Scottish Borders, and a third in London. They would have the added benefit of being fundraisers for the Yamaa Trust.

Organising these three events was a massive undertaking and I was grateful to be able to delegate this to three teams who would, I was certain, put on terrific events and hopefully give me a big lift as I ran through these regions.

Route planning was difficult. I chose a route that took in as many of the sights I really wanted to see even if this meant detours or awkward roads/trails or a few extra hills. There would need to be an element of flexibility as this was a winter run, and there were likely to be road blockages due to the snow in the mountains of Spain and Morocco. Essentially I marked points on the map that I wanted to pass. These included Loch Ness, the West Highland Way, Stirling, Edinburgh, the Scottish Borders, York, London, the Loire valley, the Pyrenees, Andalusia, The Rif Mountains, The High Atlas Mountains and Merzouga. All I had to do was figure out a rough route that connected all these places!

Injuries and illness were an obvious concern. While doing moderate, and even strenuous exercise is good for the body, too much of it can strain it beyond its limits. Staying injury free would be impossible. Accepting that I was going to have to run with some discomfort and working to limit the damage was the name of the game. Repairing and rehabilitating each injury as it occurred would maximise my chances of reaching Africa. My two most feared enemies were overuse injuries, and anaemia. The body adapts to increasing amounts of running, but I didn't know of anyone who had run so many ultra marathons consecutively, without allowing any recovery days. Stress fractures, where repetitive forces cause bones (most commonly in the lower leg and foot) to break, and inflammation of the soft tissues and tendons of the legs causing severe pain and swelling, could spell a premature end to the challenge.

Becoming severely anaemic would also finish the run. The word anaemia comes from the Greek word for lack of blood. It occurs when the body has a lower concentration of red cells, which carry oxygen from the lungs to the tissues. The red cell numbers drop when either not enough are produced, or too many are destroyed. Running long distances often causes increased destruction of red cells, lost through the trauma of the feet striking the ground repetitively, as well as increasing loss of these cells in the urine, and from the bowels.

A windy start to Scotland to Sahara in John O'Groats.

With Jennie having packed for the start.

When insufficient oxygen is transported it can lead to profound fatigue, and an inability to exercise to the same level. Iron is a key ingredient in making red blood cells. It would be impossible to make bread without flour, and likewise, iron is vital to make red blood cells. I therefore decided to take an iron containing vitamin tablet for the duration of the challenge knowing that I'd previously made myself anaemic when running monster distances. Decent footwear was called for, and I settled on UK Gear PT 1000's as a well cushioned and resilient shoe. I calculated I would need 10 pairs of shoes and I felt like a centipede when I collected them all.

I always planned to run the Indo Ultra. This 230km 6-stage race in one of the most beautiful but climactically difficult places on the planet was scheduled to finish a week before *Scotland2Sahara*. I had toyed with the idea of starting in Edinburgh, and allowing an extra week to recover, but figured missing out on Loch Ness and the West Highland Way was a bit like visiting Egypt and not going to the Pyramids.

My plan was simple. I'd run in Indonesia then take a week to recover, which would allow a maximum of 85 days to run 2659 miles to the Sahara, and get back home to Scotland in time for my wedding. But there were complications – it required military precision to calculate how I would arrive in Edinburgh on the correct day for a Sports Medical exam I was due to sit, but all these different factors would stop me from getting bored. Sacrificing either the exam or the Indo Ultra seemed like a cop out, and I was confident we could make it work.

CHAPTER 2

John O'Groats to Dunbeath

"Running makes me feel like a bird let out of a cage."
PRISCILLA WELCH

My mum wished me luck, with a look that betrayed both pride and concern. Whatever I've done in life, she's always supported me, and wild horses couldn't have kept her away from the start line in John O'Groats, but her concerns were well justified. I had lost 3.5 kg in weight in the previous few days having picked up a tummy bug in Indonesia and I'd spent an unhealthy portion of the previous night on the toilet. My eyes were sunken, and I looked cadaverous.

Simply starting was a relief, and a terrific boost. We had planned and ruminated about this moment for months, and I immediately felt liberated from the shackles of planning. Priscilla Welch commented that "running makes me feel like a bird let out of a cage," and I found myself thinking of this sentiment as I left John O'Groats. The town of John O'Groats is a tourist trap. Famous as being the most northerly inhabited place on the British mainland, great play is made of this, and a local photographer even charges to put a pole up indicating distances to nicer places that are far away.

It was great to get moving. I love running, and despite my rampantly overactive digestive system and the weather being on fast forward, I was off. This most northerly section buffeted me with a barrage of hail and sleet. With this and the spanking headwind I felt I was under attack from the elements. Huge waves smashed into dramatic cliffs. It was magnificently wild.

The first few day. Photos – Mary Murray

Day 1   Scotland 2 Sahara Blog

I must admit when i stood on the start line, at he end of the pier in john o groats with massive waves breaking over the harbour wall i didnt expect anything different. some of you may know i ran the indo ultra (a 230 km jungle race) a week before starting (and manged to place first, in a small field) so knew i was still recovering a bit from that. the combination of a severe weather warning (gales and rain) meaning a fierce headwind and an unwelcome cold/ diarrhoea virus was a tricky start, although the weather and the virus have mellowed since then. running along the A9 getting puddled by each passing lorry is far from pleasant running conditions, and im delighted to have now left the A9 behind. the amount of feedback and support ive had has been phenomenal, thanks to everyone that has sent messages on FB/ twitter/ texts, and in particular thanks loads to Dave for manning the van, fi mitchell and mike + julie for food/ warmth and banter, and Ross county for the strips, support, and help.

The headwind slowed things considerably, with those first 38 miles taking seven and a half hours. That included toilet breaks in double figures and a few spells in the van trying to warm up. The kilt I had started in lasted only the first six miles, due to it being blown up continually by the wind. With 2620 miles, or 100 marathons to go more of this would be a nightmare, I thought. The wind had apparently taken the roofs off several buildings in the Highlands, so we didn't risk popping the top of the campervan and I slept in a B+B in Dunbeath having been fortified with a family size portion of pasta from chef Dave. I spent a surreal few minutes talking about the run, but mostly debating wedding plans on BBC World Service with Jennie, who hoped that the wind would drop by February, in time for the wedding. My mind wandered, the conditions could not have been further removed from those in sunny Indonesia.

Interview with Richard Else at the start. Photo – Mary Murray

CHAPTER 3

The Indonesian Jungle Ultra

"Welcome to the Jungle."

GUNS 'N' ROSES

A week previously, I'd arrived tired and peeing blood at the finish of the Indo Ultra. When sweating buckets running up hills in the oppressive humidity of the jungle, I remember thinking that Scotland in November would be a comparative treat conditions-wise. Jungle races are notorious for the destruction they wreak on the human body and the invalids that joined me at the finish looked as if they had spent months on the run. While the average tourist enjoys the volcanic vistas, diverse cultures and remote villages of this remarkable collection of islands from the relative comfort of air conditioned cars and hotels, we had raced in humidity approaching 90% all week, carried all that we were allowed to eat, and slept in tents and chicken sheds.

The competitors had originally gathered, buzzing with excitement in the beachside resort of Sengiggi, on Lombok. I'd arrived via Bali, which seemed to be like Australia without kangaroos. At least half of the tourists were surfboard carrying Aussies, and Victoria Bitter and Steve Irwin sound-a-likes were everywhere. I could hardly sleep due to the humidity, having elected to take a non air-conditioned room to help me acclimatise. "Welcome to the Jungle" belted out on the radio, while Mt Rinjani loomed over the island of Lombok as we sailed towards it. Daniel, from Melbourne, was busy filling every vomit bag the boat possessed as we docked under coconut palms. The colour in his cheeks mirrored the foliage that spilt down towards the sea.

In addition to running, I'd helped establish the medical team, comprising a colleague, Duncan Goodall from Marathon Medical Services, and Att, who described himself as an Indonesian disaster management and mountain doctor! As Duncan's flight was delayed, Att and I checked the kit, updated the risk assessment, and discussed roles with the first aiders and other volunteers. This was to be the first ultra marathon in Indonesia, and the locals seemed quite excited by this. A film crew were following the race, and the governor of Lombok would wave us off. We were proudly told of Barack Obama's Indonesian heritage. Apparently he had spent four years at school in Jakarta, and still enjoys the ubiquitous local specialty of meatball soup. As an inaugural event, the numbers had been kept deliberately low, but an eclectic mix including British, Australian, Singaporese, Indonesian and Germans looked at the course maps we had been given. It was a completely uncompromising route, and worthy of the hushed tones that descended over the group of runners.

With the medical support established, I set about carbohydrate loading. This is important before any marathon, but especially before a multi stage self-sufficiency race, where the competitor must carry all his food. I presumed the staff had queued to watch me stuff down my fifth portion of rice, until the waiter couldn't contain his mirth any longer and asked me why I was eating the bones in the frogs legs I had ordered. The Indonesians must fear the Scots as a nation of savages with their bone eating ways, and after two further bowls of frogs legs, five rices, two bowls of meatball soup and three deserts eaten in more conventional style I sloped off to bed. President Obama was correct about the soup.

The first day was the beach day, running heavily laden along the shore to a camp that seemed to get ever further away. The conditions were terminal for any prospect of a quick time, with the only relief from the hot sun coming from the multiple river crossings. 39km and 4 hours 7mins later, I leapt over several fishing lines that had doubled as tripwires for runners and crossed the line. I felt like death warmed up, and then microwaved, and evidently everyone else felt the same, judging by the smiles of pure relief on their faces when they crossed the line. It had felt like considerably more than 39kms though the sand, and I was almost pleased we'd be ascending onto the sacred Mt Rinjani the next day.

Refreshing jungle shower. Photo – Rieka Goodall

Doctor Duncan Goodall cools a competitor down. Photo – Rieka Goodall

Gunung Rinjani at 3726 metres dominates Lombok and has earned considerable spiritual gravitas with the locals who describe it in hushed tones. Its slopes gradually wind through settlements and then the cloud forest before steepening to emerge with views of the crater and its steely blue lake beneath. The village of Senaru clings to its slopes and a steep downhill from our high point sling-shotted us through thick jungle into the stick fighting capital of Indonesia. This traditional art pits the two combatants against each other, armed with shields and sticks. Points are scored for hits on various parts of the body and there was no chance I was taking the locals on at this. I reckon Senaru probably boasts the world's largest population of roosters, and an infuriating cacophony of cock-a-doodle-dooing ensured minimal sleep for all but the profoundly deaf.

Despite the lack of sleep, Day Three involved a bewitching descent to the coconut zone at sea level, through jungle, rice paddies, and tobacco fields, before shooting up the opposite side of the mountain through the monkey forest and emerging onto alpine slopes. The 20-odd kilometres up the hill was the most aggressive heat I've ever run in, far outstripping the Sahara, and forcing a slow jog. Word came through that everyone was struggling, and the road was completely melted in parts. Even the hugely experienced Jo Kilkenny had to call it quits due to the heat. There are over 17,000 islands in Indonesia and Lombok must be its most exhilarating. Surf beaches and world class diving beckoned, but it would be another three days hard running before we'd get near these treats. Some of the competitors already appeared to have more blisters than Indonesia has islands. Others hobbled around on swollen tendons, sore backs, and a variety of other maladies. However there was not a rooster in sight, and a spectacular campsite set the scene for an explosion of colour as the sun set over the still active, volcanic shoulders of Mt Rinjani.

I'd built up a healthy lead and slept well. Day Four offered ageless agricultural scenes, skimming over narrow paths between chilli farms, paddy fields and tobacco plantations before following the shrieks of the monkeys up through a high pass. The climb was considerably less arduous than the previous day's and I almost skipped up knowing a swinging downhill waited. This section found a road, and I took pride in racing a truck stacked with coconuts, overtaking and being overtaken as it lurched down hairpin bends. The truck won eventually, and I settled for a recovery drink at camp, before having a game of football with the local kids, taking a wash that my stench dictated as compulsory in the pleasant confines of a waterfall, and patching up other competitor's blisters. A 'flatter' 47kms day lay in wait, although the route profile still resembled the back of a Stegosaurus. This whipped past numerous villages, each a relative metropolis compared to the rooster HQ of Senaru. Shopkeepers bustled and hustled, while water buffalo and goats grazed. Just as the end seemed to be imminent, a marshall informed me that a bridge was down, and we'd have to divert a further few kilometres. This felt like a kick where it hurt, and the following 40 minutes was the hardest of the week.

Camp was next to an idyllic pond housing countless fish in the middle of the jungle. Losing an ongoing war with the local insect population and finding some king sized spiders diminished the joy of kicking back in a hammock. Instead I chatted to Karen Hathaway, and compared this to racing in the UK. Karen is used to taking on and beating the men at ultra distance and, like me, she was finding the heat a distinct menace. She'd picked up several injuries but still ran strongly, declaring that this was to "find some water and shade as soon as possible. You don't want to be out there any longer than you have to."

I reflected on this, and ran the first section with Karen the next day before accelerating as the heat cranked up. I thought of the two German lads and felt guilty about moaning to myself. They were carrying a tripod and taking photos all the way round. I never saw anything other than a smile on their faces, or heard anything more other than "das ist gut" from them. Nick, who I'd shared a tent with looked as if he had swapped one of his ankles with an elephant. Perhaps to emphasise that no-one escapes the jungle unscathed, I began to pee blood. It was not the first time this had happened, but was comfortably the reddest my pee has ever been, looking like cherryade. Sadly this somewhat tempered my elation at finishing this magnificent challenge in first place. For all the wonderful sunsets, the cultural interaction, and the new party trick that so impressed the doctors, peeing blood and being physically wrecked wasn't classic preparation for the biggest challenge of my life.

But my biggest challenge had to be put in context. In Indonesia, there is the ever present threat of natural disaster. Arriving back to civilisation, the newspapers were abuzz with news that Mt Merapi on Java had erupted, and that over 350 people had perished. The television showed lava and ash bursting out repeatedly and revealed that 350,000 people had been evacuated. Our colleague Att, had been called away with the disaster management team. Att explained that unfortunately natural disasters are a fact of life in Indonesia, and are relatively common. Of these, the most famous were the 1883 eruption of Krakatoa in which over 120,000 are believed to have died, and an entire island vanished, and the 2004 Boxing Day earthquake and subsequent tsunami which measured 9.1 on the Richter scale, the third largest ever, when more than 230,000 lives were lost, more than half of these in Indonesia. Having taken some of this in, I let my family know I was safe, and went to bed stunned. I attempted some exam revision having emptied the hotel's coffee supply into my stomach. Despite Indonesia being home to some of the world's best coffee, the label read "sourced responsibly from Kenya."

Football in a rice paddy. Photo – Rieka Goodall

CHAPTER 4

Dunbeath to Kinlochleven

"There is no such thing as bad weather, only inappropriate clothing."

My dodgy guts were an unwanted souvenir from Indonesia. Day Two of *Scotland2Sahara* brought less wind, and the antibiotics I had taken for my stomach bug had started to work. The TV the night before had shown footage of Mt Merapi's continued eruptions but here in the highlands glorious sunshine burst out at times. To confirm we were still in Scotland, Dave and I had some chips and Irn-Bru in Helmsdale. This was far removed from the nutritional strategy I had spent months drawing up, but it went down like a wet penguin. The proprietor had assured Dave they were "fresh cut," and "not any of that packet rubbish."

Undulating moorland and castles were the order of the day. Thirty six miles brought us past Dunrobin Castle and its legendary birds of prey, and then the small town of Golspie, and a bed for the night at my friend Fi Mitchell's. I read about the notorious "Stalin of Scotland," the 1st Duke of Sutherland who evicted thousands from his lands whilst erecting an enormous and impressive monument to himself on nearby Ben Bhraggie. He sounded like a very bad egg to me, although Dunrobin Castle, his former house has a more generous account of him on their website describing George Granville Leveson-Gower, Duke of Sutherland as "liberal and reforming," whilst acknowledging his role in the Sutherland clearances. I failed to do much exam revision and felt as weak as Fi's kitten Hobbes as I forced down lashings of a splendid spaghetti bolognese, and headed for bed at 9pm.

Friends on the West Highland Way

Family run on the Great Glen Way

I'd slept like the dead, and Fi joined me for a crisp morning's jog, and a bout of truck dodging. The area around Loch Fleet, and south to Inverness, is full of beauty and character, but its main road, the A9, is no friend of the runner. I'd previously run the length of Scotland doing more miles a day than I was currently, while suffering virtually no injuries. This time however, my left Achilles tendon was already swollen and sore. I'm certain that running on the busy single carriageway road, with a steep camber and a verge that was impossible to run on was causing this. I did try the verge on occasion only succeeding in looking like a drunk as I stumbled through shin deep grass on uneven ground, before retreating to the lunacy of jogging on the A9 which according to former SNP leader John Swinney has "the disgraceful accolade of being Scotland's most dangerous road," and has "also been classified as one of its least popular." 26% of Scots had voted the A9 their least favourite road, and it was streets ahead in my estimation, although I haven't sampled the delights of running the A96, which pipped the A9 by a couple of votes in the most recent "least favourite road in Scotland" poll.

For a country that had invented the television, penicillin and indeed tarmac itself, surely we could come up with a better road than this. I imagined John MacAdam turning in his grave, and refreshed my memory on treatment of Achilles tendon problems while eating pasta cooked by the attentive Dave. My book told me how to treat Achilles Tendinopathy – rest was at the top of the list. This was not what I had in mind for the next 80 odd days, so I'd have to find routes that were kinder on the legs, cut my distance slightly to 32 miles today, and ice and elevate my legs when I finished each day.

All I could do in addition was hope and pray that these measures would limit the extent of any discomfort.

Fortunately my cousin Scott Morrison plays for the Dingwall football team Ross County. He'd arranged a press shoot and some ice and painkillers for our arrival in Dingwall and it was great to catch up and have some friendly banter with Scott and team mascot Staggie. Eight foot in height and resplendent with king sized antlers, I declined the offer of running in the Staggie costume for the following day's leg, and Scott ignored my offer of giving the Ross County team the *S2S* route maps if they fancied some hard pre-season training. Although I'm an Aberdeen fan, I'd been to see County several times when I'd lived in Inverness and it was pleasing on the legs to be on turf rather than the road, although my football skills are more Madonna than Maradona.

The route for Day Four was magnificent. It clambered up a back road onto high ground to yield unsurpassed views down onto the mighty Loch Ness itself. Snow covered mountains reared up behind the Loch but despite the beautiful scenery I was miserable. Both my Achilles were now sore, so much so that every step induced hefty pain in that region, and what felt like a dagger through my heart. How could I go on like this? There was still over 2500 miles to go. Why was this happening? I'd run much further before. Dave cheered me up. He would be leaving today having been there since the start. We agreed that any proceeds from monster spotting would go to the Yamaa Trust, although I felt there was more chance of a glimpse of the fabled Loch Ness Monster than me successfully arriving in Morocco. In retrospect this was one of the low points of the trip and I felt pathetic. That day I'd only managed 27.4 miles, which would prove to be the lowest of the entire venture. If I failed this challenge I would be letting so many people down. I had two choices – to give up, or to sort myself medically, and the mental battle would take care of itself. My friends Mike and Julie hadn't seen the monster either, but they did have sympathy, a comfortable bed, some ice for my legs, and an outstanding paella for dinner. I ruminated for several hours wallowing in my misery prior to eventually managing to get some shut-eye.

The following two days offered an unrivalled opportunity for dog walking, carrying myself, and at times my mum and dad's dog Ben, along the trail routes of the Great Glen Way, and then onto the West Highland Way. The Great Glen Way follows a massive fault line that carves Scotland in two. High mountains loom over the trail although they were invisible in the perma-drizzle that blessed these two days. I had placed cardboard heel raises in my shoes and that seemed to offload some of the pressure from my Achilles and I enjoyed the prospect of being splashed only by myself, as opposed to the joys of the A9 where every passing truck happily obliged. The sense of brooding history was tangible at each settlement I passed and mum and dad kept me fed and watered while I kept Ben well exercised. Ben continued to look daisy fresh despite clocking up some good mileage. I only managed 28 and 29.5 miles respectively on days five and six but felt happier in myself. I was out in the wilds of Scotland, and my Achilles tendons were getting no worse. Not even Fort William could literally dampen my spirits. Huddling in the shadow of Ben Nevis, Fort William receives the most rain of any town in the UK. It averages 200mm each November, and was getting much of this in sleet when I passed through. I had intended climbing Ben Nevis via Carn Mor Dearg in addition to my run that day, but canned the idea due to my Achilles problems. This seemed a shrewd move as I hot-footed it along the West Highland Way to Kinlochleven, running flat out to keep warm through the wind, snow and torrents of water that blasted down off the Mamore mountains. I passed an army team who had been up on the Mamores, but had beat a retreat due to conditions. In the five minutes I stopped to chat to them I was frozen. It was a far cry from a couple months previous when I'd run the Mamores with Joe Symonds on a day the visibility was described as "superb" on the mountain weather forecast. A wise man once said, "there is no such thing as bad weather, only inappropriate clothing." This was bad weather and I was glad to reach civilisation and the Tailrace Inn at Kinlochleven.

CHAPTER 5

The West Highland Way Race

"One Step Closer To Home."

I love Kinlochleven. Soaring peaks surround the village and even when the weather disappoints, the climbing wall and pub do not. My friends Geraldine and Stuart were putting me up for the night, and the village was full of people doing 'the *S2S* Ultra' the next day. The Tailrace Inn was buzzing with talk of snow blocking the route, running injuries, and football scores. I was given heel pads, ice packs, and a pint of lager to ease any pain that existed in my tendons, with excellent results. This was more than could be said for the Scotland rugby team, which was getting dismantled by New Zealand. Catching up with Jennie over the telephone had kept me sane. It had distracted me from the run and the books, as so much else was going on. We had all the major issues covered for the wedding, but there was still the honeymoon, the house we were to move into after our wedding, and plenty besides to work through. I was amazed she was staying sane, as she told me of everything she had on her plate. I thought of the classic image of a swan appearing entirely calm, but with its feet motoring like crazy beneath the surface of the water.

This part of the West Highland Way is rugged and spectacular. I thought it would be a superb day for people to join me for a run and it turned out to be one of the best days of the trip. I'd set up the *Scotland2Sahara* run to challenge myself and enjoy the scenery at the same time. I also hoped to encourage others to do likewise, and could additionally spread the word about the Yamaa Trust. The World Health Organisation currently recommends 150 minutes of moderate

The S2S Ultra, runners joined in a day of the challenge. Kinlochleven to Tyndrum. Photo – Mary Murray

exercise, or 75 minutes of strenuous exercise per week, to keep healthy, and this was another opportunity to emphasize the benefits of exercise to the media. A lack of activity is probably the biggest single risk factor in limiting life expectancy in the UK. A presentation by Dr Steven Boyce, a Sports and Exercise Medicine doctor from Glasgow hammered home to me that by keeping active (and only 35-45% of us hit current recommendations,) we are significantly lowering our risk of heart attacks, stroke, lung problems, diabetes, some cancers, obesity, depression, and much more besides. It is interesting that amongst doctors, and other health care professionals, exercise is now recognised as a medicine, and is increasingly being 'prescribed,' with clear instructions to the patient. It's a mark of how important exercise and activity is regarded that Sports and Exercise Medicine is now a medical speciality in its own right, like Orthopaedics or Cardiology. The government seems set to invest significantly in addressing the problem of the nation's inactivity, by setting and hitting targets in a similar manner to the way they are encouraging awareness of the health problems of smoking and alcohol. Amen to that.

The event organisers Sandbaggers and Tribesport had worked tirelessly to encourage friends, family, and people who had heard of the challenge to run, and to set up the safety and medical cover, and all else that is required to put on a professionally staged event. This was no small undertaking, and I was grateful I didn't have to do much of the organising. With the Sandbaggers team's expertise in putting races on, the organisation was first class, and the weather superb. A motley crew of 70 assembled in bright sunshine on the start line for the 28 mile run. This included top international runners such as Jethro Lennox, Joe Symonds and Richie Cunningham as well as the full A-Team and over 30 people in kilts. Unfortunately Papa Smurf was absent, having failed to get time off work – Smurfing working time directives must be unduly restrictive.

The West Highland Way runs through Kinlochleven, and the long distance trail is a mecca for ultramarathon runners. Three major events a year take place on this wonderland of mountains, moor and lochs. Of these, the biggest challenge, run annually in June, is found in completing its 95 miles, to include 4450 metres of ascent in one go. The West Highland Way Race began in 1985 when Duncan Watson and Bobby Shields had a 'discussion' as to who was the fittest runner, and pledged to settle this dispute by competing over the ground from Glasgow to Fort William. As race organiser Stan Bland points out, the etymology of the word 'competition' is interesting, derived from the Latin word 'competare' – to strive together. Watson and Shields apparently went at it hammer and tongs until they decided to shake hands at the Devil's Staircase, more than 70 miles in and helped each other to complete the distance. Almost every runner that has pitted their body against the course describes a spirit of mutual respect and friendship amongst the 175 runners that start the race each year. Remarkably, Jez Bragg has completed the course in 15 hours 44 minutes but typical of the spirit of the race, Jez is on record as saying he has the greatest of respect and admiration for runners who brave the cold and midges for two nights, in a bid to finish within the cut-off time of 36 hours.

Typically of Scotland and the highlands in particular, the weather during the race can be highly variable. Blizzards on the hilltops are not uncommon, and the race has even been stopped because of flash floods. Cases of heatstroke have been confirmed, while in other years the suggested five complete changes of clothes have been used. Most runners describe the experience as veering between torture and bliss.

An integral element of the West Highland Way Race is the support crew. Stan Bland describes such crew as "typically going 48hours without sleep, getting abused and appreciated in equal measure." Most runners argue that the challenge is a team event, with the support crew as important as the athletes themselves. Runner Bill Heirs acknowledged that "without them, there would be no race," and as I reached the West Highland Way, I reflected on the unstinting support I'd enjoyed so far, and it's necessity for the rest of the route to Morocco. For the project to succeed, I relied upon the goodwill and patience of these unsung heroes. Attempting to run to Morocco completely unsupported through winter would be even more daunting, and being physically at the scene of this famous race brought this home to me. I'd run the race in 2008, and both adored and hated it. A long

S2S Ultra. Yamaa Trust fundraiser, and to emphasize the benefits of exercise. Photos – Mary Murray

single stage race was a new and eye-opening experience for me, but the sense of anticipation amongst competitors and their support crews was the equal of any race I have subsequently run. I'd set off looking to complete the distance in 19 or 20 hours, and bounded towards the shores of Loch Lomond over the iconic Conic Hill. My esteem for the course was further enhanced by the hot dogs, hot chocolates, baked potatoes, and other food offered to me by other runner's support crews. I grasped what a truly remarkable race this was, not only due to the scale of the challenge, and grandeur of the location, but the unshakable encouragement of all involved.

Pain is embraced, and almost treasured in retrospect by all that run ultra marathons. Many will claim it helps them feel alive, and will run as close to their personal pain threshold as possible. For me, the realisation that I still had 20 miles left struck me immediately when I felt a pop in my right foot. This foot, which had been niggling became bitterly afflictive, and made me take my shoe off to have a look. Pressing over the bone was tender, and I knew I'd stress fractured a metatarsal. Stress fractures are caused by repeated or unusual pressure exerted upon a bone, in contrast to the more common fractures, caused by an excessive impact force. The metatarsals are a row of bones in the mid-foot that are amongst the most common sites for stress fractures. By the finish, having slowed considerably, which merely prolonged my anguish, I was tired and had a foot so swollen I couldn't put my shoe back on. I'd underestimated the training required, and it felt as though I'd been carried to the finish less by my own ill functioning legs, but by the support of other competitors and crew. I'd finished in 23 hrs 20 mins, a full 6 hours behind the winner and could only admire the guts of those braving a second night without sleep in their bid to reach Fort William. My foot and fatigue had left me with the mood and patience of a wild rhinoceros, but this softened when I heard the stories of hardship and endurance by other competitors.

Mark Hamilton, running in 2006, had fractured his ankle after only five miles. He is clearly a more determined man than me, surviving the remaining 90 miles on a mixture of banter, food and painkillers. Reading his story about his epic regard for the race, and his thirst to finish, sent a shiver down my spine, similar to the one experienced on the start line. I've broken my ankle on 3 occasions (none of them running), and can say categorically there is no chance I'd have run 90 miles with Mark's injury. Adrian Davis, a winner in 2007 who I ran with at the Everest Marathon, feels, "it's a challenge just to finish in one piece, but to all who endeavour to try it, be prepared mentally and physically for a fantastic challenge." He claims that meticulous preparation maximises chances of success, and that finishing is within the compass of all those who prepare.

Ultra runner and sports medical doctor Steve Boyce completed the West Highland Way race in 2002. He suggests that, "it's difficult to describe, but people who have done the race will understand. I was sore, hallucinating (through lack of sleep) and behaving irrationally. It nearly killed me, but at the finish, I felt I could have run further. It's the next day that the pain really kicked in."

He offers an intriguing perspective on the psychology of endurance running.

"Of course you need to have a high level of physical fitness to participate in these events but there is no doubt that the mind plays a significant part in ultra running. It's often stated that in a 100-mile race you run the first 50 miles with your legs, and the second 50 miles with your head. Invariably everyone who completes one of these races, from the top finishers to those at the back of the pack will all have had a bad spell at some point in the race where they 'lose it in the head'. It's how you cope with this, combined with the pain and suffering that gets you the finisher's medal.

All runners will have their individual strategies for coping. To take my mind off the thought of running continuously for such a long distance, I try and break the event down into a series of shorter sections. Another trick is to forget about time. Put your watch in your pocket and just run as to how you feel. Constantly checking your watch can make you feel stressed if you've not reached your planned split times. As I fatigue progressively and start suffering, one song always goes through my mind. 'One Step Closer To Home' by the Alarm… "the tougher it gets, the harder it is, I'm one step closer to home."

Steve continues, "As a runner, I hate being injured. As we speak, I'm four days away from an ankle operation, but I'm not letting it bother me. I am training on the exercise bike and am more concerned with the fact that five weeks later I have, on consecutive weekends, the West Highland Way Race, and two major runs in the Alps. Why continue? Why do you do these runs? Why do ultras? All are reasonable questions that family members, other runners, physiotherapists and orthopaedic surgeons have asked me over the years. These are difficult questions to answer and if I'm honest I don't know why. It's not for success as I haven't won anything since the late nineties. The only answer that I can truthfully offer is the self satisfaction of competing in these events."

Steve's words strike a chord with me. Running with a bit of pain is tolerable. Not to be able to run would be intolerable. Injury is complete misery.

CHAPTER 6

Kinlochleven to Edinburgh

*"Oi big man, are you the one
running tae Africa,"*

The full West Highland Way Race runs in the opposite direction to that we would be taking for the *S2S* ultra. The weather was considerably colder than when I'd run the full race but the *S2S* was blessed with a sublime winter's day. Having the opportunity to make, and catch up with so many friends was fantastic. I knew I would have ample opportunity to familiarise myself with the loneliness of the long distance runner as I ventured further south, and the weather and company, as well as being on this most beautiful of courses, without a broken foot was a bonus. I chatted happily to Rab Lee as we climbed out of Kinlochleven, the pair of us resplendent in kilts. Rab quickly had me in fits of laughter discussing a multitude of capers, and we somehow managed to get lost, forcing a further yomp though snow covered bogs high above Glen Coe. I quickly realised there are issues with running over snow-covered bogs when wearing a kilt that can make grown men scream. A friend, Donnie Campbell, had questioned my sense of direction, saying I'd probably end up in Russia rather than Morocco, and it took us a while to get back on track. When I phoned Donnie to tell him I'd got lost I could hear him howling with laughter. Eating up the miles through the atmospheric Glen Coe, and the desolate Rannoch Moor while bantering with friends, dressed variously as Vikings, Crusaders, and Hannibal was a real tonic, and my only regret was because of my diversion I missed Batman playing the bagpipes at the start of the shorter seven mile run.

Family and friends on the West Highland Way. Photos – Mary Murray

A further 70 people were taking on the shorter but equally picturesque run from Bridge of Orchy to Tyndrum and it was wonderful to see 140 folk in all taking on the difficult but awe-inspiring terrain, and getting a taste of what I would be doing every day for the foreseeable future. The seven miles, or 28 miles was a huge challenge for many, and most retired to the pub afterwards for well deserved refreshments. Jethro Lennox had been finished almost an hour and a half before me and was showered, had eaten and could probably have written a book by the time I arrived. My sister Susie had run the 28 miles despite twisting her ankle early on, and needed all the resilience and courage that typifies her character to arrive in Tyndrum with a smile and a tennis ball sized lump on her ankle.

The A-Team were in some state and were all limping, but brightened considerably on hearing the welcome news that the pub was less than 100 metres away. Their plan had come together and they were "loving it." Howling mad Murdock was limping like a cowboy, and BA Baracus's jewellery was falling to bits. These lads, who I'd gone to University with, had got the job done, and that's what I needed to do in the next two months. I said my all too short goodbyes to Jennie, who had run the 28 miler but had to be at work the next day, and retreated to the pub to play pool and darts and astound everyone with my ability to eat three main meals, four portions of onion rings, three desserts, and four bags of peanuts. It is difficult to articulate how heartened I was by this day, with the efforts that everyone had made, and it felt I was back in the real world.

Following Day Seven's excitement, I was running solo again on Day Eight. The thermometer read -9 degrees celcius as I crawled out of my sleeping bag and scraped the ice from the inside and outside of the campervan. The snowy scene was superb, with Ben More and Stob Binnein lit up in the early morning light like a wedding cake. My state of mind had begun to depend on the weather, and how my legs felt. The weather was ideal, crystal clear, with views for miles. Every branch twinkled with the harsh frost that had enveloped the valley. Having cleared Crianlarich, I ran onward along the shores of Loch Lomond into Rob Roy MacGregor country.

Having spent the morning admiring God's creation while slipping recurrently on ice, by midday the weather had changed to ensure I would be running on the soggy, soggy banks of Loch Lomond. I traversed the undulating and ankle breaking track around Inversnaid which is riddled with tree roots. This is the section of the West Highland Way that many runners dislike, as getting a rhythm going while clambering over trees and rocks is impossible. The local goats were having less difficulty and even perched on trees to demonstrate their agility. Whilst not quite emulating Rob Roy, the flame haired outlaw of the Hollywood films who is local to these parts, I nonetheless raided the campervan for all its cake, and made off down the road towards Stirling. 29 miles that day took me towards Aberfoyle.

While running on the road near Aberfoyle I was approached by a council truck.

"Oi big man, are you the one running tae Africa," one of the lads shouted.

"Aye, come run a bit if you like," I responded.

"I'll tell you what, ram that, but here's some money for your charity, and watch out for them blisters. My mate does marathons and he says you'll definitely get some."

Brilliant! I loved the generosity of spirit of the people of Scotland. Interactions like these continually made my day. Another Rob, MacDonald, had supported me for the day. I dropped him back to Tyndrum and drove to Aunty Sarah's in Stirling. The Wallace Monument and the castle provided a spectacular backdrop. I tried to revise, mustering two chapters of the too many I still had to read. I hope they ask plenty questions about Achilles tendons I thought. There was loads of support coming through on Facebook and Twitter which was much welcome. I had been texting through updates daily to these sites, and it seemed plenty were still stiff and sore from the *S2S* ultra. Apparently one of the lads was so stiff he was refusing to go up any stairs and couldn't put his shoes on.

Mist thicker than green pea soup blanketed Scotland the following morning. I chatted with Mike Adams, who organises the Glenmore24 race and was driving the van this day. I'd have to change route. The road to Stirling would be too dangerous even in high visibility clothing. We skirted Fintry, apparently a picture postcard village. Seeing only about the length of my arm Mike, navigated and we carried on eventually finishing at Falkirk Wheel, 34 miles from my start point, having shared some banana cake with a local cyclist. I took a lift back to Aunty Sarah's in Stirling, a place full of history, and I was sorry not to run directly through and past the iconic Wallace Monument and Stirling Castle. Feeling better, I managed a few hours revision before falling asleep and had a bizarre dream about gorillas, presumably brought on by the mist. In this dream I had refused to stop in Morocco and had carried on south to Uganda. Several gorillas, who spoke perfect English joined me for a few hours before overheating due to their fur. They sent me on my way with some bananas, and more surprisingly some Irn-Bru. Sigourney Weaver was nowhere to be seen.

The Falkirk Wheel was surprisingly impressive. A mesmerising spectacle it took Rab Lee and I a while to find a way onto the canal path to Edinburgh. Given our failure to find the obvious path up on the West Highland Way, this was no surprise. The canal path was the first properly flat day I'd had, which was a relief as there was a chunky headwind, and I had to make it to Edinburgh in time for my exam the next day. I felt awful that morning. Maybe it was the exam hanging over me, like the sword of Damacles. I ate the right things, and put one foot in front of the other, and repeated. Rab declared that the magic wand was to be found in the form of a bacon roll. The lady in the cafe had seen a newspaper article which joked I would do anything to avoid wedding preparations. She wished my fiancée well for the wedding. While I'd probably be failed in the impending exam for claiming that bacon rolls are optimal ultra marathon fuel, Rab had been spot on. After 36 miles, I was in Edinburgh and celebrated with some Irn-Bru, in honour of the gorillas.

The Falkirk Wheel

CHAPTER 7

Edinburgh to Rowley

"There is no try. Do or do not."

YODA

When most people pay a visit to Edinburgh, they tend to visit the castle, the Scottish parliament, or Holyrood House. Unfortunately my only visit outside my parent's house was to be to the exam hall at the Royal College of Surgeons. However I was a long way from being in suitable condition for this at present. 319 miles in 10 days, mostly into the prevailing south-westerly wind had left me looking like Roald Dahl's Mr Twit. Major surgery to my beard improved matters slightly, and I was advised that a bath was most certainly in order. My brother Iain, who was also sitting the exam, and I sat down for some last minute revision and a monumental pile of food (which mostly consisted of potato waffles.) Revision had been less extensive than I'd hoped and Iain openly guffawed at a couple of my answers. I had worked as hard as I could but was so fatigued each night, and so distracted with route selection and phone calls that I wasn't overly confident. Iain tried to iron some of the crinkles out of my shirt and sports medical knowledge – we had done as much as we could.

For wisdom it is difficult to look past Yoda. "There is no try. Do or do not," I think well sums up that an exam is only worth turning up for if you pass. The lucky socks went on, to garner as much confidence as was feasible in this situation, and Iain and I went to the exam. Dark clouds loomed overhead. While waiting for the other candidates to assemble I ate several bananas and some hot cross buns to catch up on calories. A terrific hush followed the chief examiner in the door, and our task was explained.

(Top left) Exiting exam and raring to get going. The Ultimate Marathon Man, Triple Echo Productions for BBC Scotland. Welcome to England. (Top right and bottom row) Photos – Jennie Murray

The exam was as nerve shredding as exams always are for me, and lasted three hours. A couple of the examiners wished me well for the rest of the run, as we exited the Royal College of Surgeons like a pair of scalded cats. I had vowed not to take a single day off, and due to the exam, it was 1.30pm before I started running that day. Not even rank weather could dampen the elation of having finished the exam. Had I passed? It was difficult to be confident, especially with a fail rate of 50% but it hadn't been a disaster. The results wouldn't be out for a couple weeks, but there were no more textbooks to be read for now. Interestingly the textbook seemed fairly clear that what I was attempting was inadvisable. The consensus was that allowing adequate time for recovery between heavy exercise was imperative, as Iain reminded me by quoting my predicted doom from the textbook.

I ran that day with Donnie Campbell and David Knox. Donnie and I do a fair bit of running together and David works for several media outlets in the borders and is a keen ultra runner. It was fun doing an interview while hurtling down the A7. Having left at 1.30 it was dark less than three hours after this. Shortly after 4pm the head torches went on and we just chatted about football, rugby and general bloke chat. It was great to have company again on what was a fairly grim afternoon in the dark, although Donnie's renditions of Cher, Tina Turner and other 'favourites' made the hills seem steeper. David was the only journalist to actually spend substantial time running with me, and later wrote the following in the Border Telegraph;

"Running, at times, needs distractions. On Thursday it was up to Donnie and me to add the distractions. And despite the horrendous conditions, the five hours of running were certainly enjoyable.

We swapped injury stories, shared our thoughts on footwear, talked down our running achievements (I didn't have any), tried to imagine the worst foods you can eat, and discussed lots of bloke stuff. Running through Gorebridge and Middleton was tough as we jostled for a narrow lane on the A7 with the continuous traffic. But relief was to be found as we cut off the main road at Heriot. For the next three or so hours we joked and laughed our way down to Stow then over to Clovenfords. Marriage advice, the joys of being called Andy Murray, and Donnie's new girlfriend kept the mood light through the descending darkness. One thing you need for ultra running is a sense of humour and Andy and Donnie are both well equipped."

These were to be a hectic few days, and after finishing that night I hot-footed it to the Melrose Rugby club, home of the oldest Rugby Sevens tournament in the world, who were hosting a fundraising night. The Scottish Borders had been my home for the last three years, and the turnout was fantastic. It amazed and humbled me how many people had been following the run, and to hear stories that people had been inspired to get out and do some exercise by my efforts. I'd had an email from Charles Gordon, who had committed to go for a run every day I was on the road, maybe he would even run further than me!

Training with Donnie Campbell. Donnie recently ran from Glasgow to Skye non stop

It was hilarious listening to ex-Scotland rugby star Craig Chalmers describing walking with Ian Botham during his epic Lands End to John O'Groats charity walk, and the unusual line of refreshments they would indulge in. What could be better, great food, old friends, and another great fundraiser for the Yamaa Trust, masterminded by the vivacious Elise and Malcolm Ross. Melrose's physiotherapist Dougie was kind enough to give me a quick massage, and made up some potions for me. For about the first time ever, I took a lift for the 800 metres from the rugby club to my house at the foot of the Eildon Hills.

I slept in my own bed that night. There was something innately satisfying about this, especially given that this visit to Melrose, with my upcoming wedding, was the last time I could truly call it home. It's a wonderful, congenial town, nestled on the banks of the Tweed, with its ancient Gothic Abbey founded by Cistercian monks in 1136.

Melrose Abbey

The abbey is incredible, not only for its sweeping architecture, widely regarded as some of the finest in Britain, but also for its rich tapestry of history. The heart of Robert the Bruce, one of Scotland's greatest kings, and the greatest warrior of his generation is buried in the abbey grounds. I had been intrigued to find out that the Bruce's heart had followed a similar route to the one I would take. Robert the Bruce was belligerent, as characterised by his refusal to meet the English forces on their terms, always meeting on uneven ground, adopting an almost guerrilla style to his warfare. The battle of Bannockburn in 1314 saw the English army trapped, then defeated, and Scotland gain functional independence. Years late, the Bruce, realising his death was imminent, ordered his heart to be embalmed and taken on crusade by his friend James Douglas.

The Black Douglas, as he was known, made it as far as Andalusia where he was killed. The Bruce's death bed instructions, for his heart to be returned to Melrose Abbey were respected, and it remains there to this day. I'd followed the history of the Bruce from Bannockburn to Melrose, and would pass through Andalusia on my way to Morocco.

A legendary tale describes Robert the Bruce in hiding following several defeats. He is said to have watched a spider spinning a web, attempting a seemingly impossible connection between two areas of a cave. Countless times the web failed, until finally the spider succeeded. The Bruce took this as an omen, and renewed his efforts to achieve independence for Scotland. This tale is often cited to illustrate the benefits of perseverance, and I well remember my mum describing it to me in Kenya when I was a youngster aged six or so, saying "if at first you don't succeed, try, try, try again." I frequently thought of the spider, and its tenacity of purpose during my run. There would be setbacks, but accepting this, and persisting to find a way to achieve my goal would separate completion from failure.

Cocooned in my own bed, I could have slept for months. Instead it was the earliest start of the whole trip, and I grabbed a lift back with Dad to where I'd finished the night before. At 7am I got moving to allow me to run a couple miles and arrive at the correct juncture for the planned fun run at 7.30. My good friend Ian Reilly had organised a packed programme in the Scottish Borders to coincide with my run. Over 60 hardy souls, some of whom had never run before, braved the cold and early morning for the fun run. Ages ranged from 70 years of age to the youngest Seb managing 6kms at three months, although he did get some help from his mum Rachel. To 'run' this distance in 32 minutes at three months of age must be a record in that age category! Marshalls from Gala Harriers led the field safely to the Hospital for snacks, and to catch up with old friends who had put on bacon rolls, and brought some cakes for me to take with me. The showers at the hospital must have been packed, as staff piled in following the run. Accident and Emergency looked as busy as ever but I wasn't offering to stay and help out on this occasion. An ex-colleague caught me at one point. "You running again Andrew, where are you off to?" he asked.

"Bonchester Bridge today, but I'm actually jogging down to Morocco" I replied.

"Best of luck with that, probably beats night shift."

From there, it was on to Melrose Primary where, due to the presence of the TV cameras, I got quite a reception. Every one of the 340 pupils joined me for a lap or two of the playground, and several asked me why I was running so slowly. For the 200 metre circuit, the kids would race despite the protestations of the staff to "go canny," and the quickest Primary 7 kids were home and hosed by the time I was half way round. Councillor Alasdair Hutton, who had been a very fine runner in his youth, competing with the likes of the great Herb Elliot, said many kind words. His tales of Herb Elliot interested me hugely, as I'd read much of the flying Australian, who never tasted defeat over 1500 metres. Through his coach Percy Cerutty, Elliot sought diverse role models including Da Vinci and Jesus, and seemed to train more naturally than his contemporaries, working out mostly in the Melbourne suburbs and beaches.

The pupils had brought me some very thoughtful presents, most of which I ate, but the clothing and posters accompanied me to the finish line. It was extremely touching, and one particular hat, complete with flaps, saved my ears from freezing several times. My favourite poster remained on display in the van until the finish in Morocco. The schedule was extremely tight that day, and I sped off through the mist in the direction of Lilliesleaf Primary School. Cresting the hill, the clouds were below me and I was tempted to nip up the Eildon Hills where I had run most often in training. I'd probably run different routes in those hills 150 times in the previous year, and not going up them felt as if I was passing a close friend's house and not going in. I felt frightfully rude, but had to press on. The reception at Lilliesleaf was fantastic, and I really enjoyed the infectious enthusiasm and singing of the kids. By this time a couple days solidly on my feet had caused my Achilles' to look like sticks of rhubarb. Even when I wasn't running, I had been standing. My legs felt as if they were seizing up. I pressed on to Hawick, accompanied by Terni on a bike. They must have been the slowest miles of the trip, I could hardly move. Following a stimulating chat with pupils at Hawick High, we were off to the Teviot Medical Centre.

With pupils from Melrose Primary School. Photo – Scott Murray   *Colleagues at Teviot Medical Practice*

The Eildon Hills

I'd worked at the Teviot for a year immediately prior to the run, and had gained the reputation as a big eater. During the challenge, to sustain the 34 odd miles a day through the variable terrain that I would be running, I had calculated I would need to eat between 7000 and 8000 Kcal per day. That is more than three times the usual requirement of a normal man, and it had been quite an effort forcing enough food down to sustain my weight. To reach 7800Kcal, if I ate only Weetabix, I would need to eat 128 Weetabix a day, or if I obtained all calories from bread, I would need to gobble 3.1kg per day. The Teviot baking corps had rustled up enough food for a rogue elephant and I set about this delicious task with gusto. Most of my ex-colleagues seemed mildly horrified by the state of my Achilles tendons. I think privately several had reservations as to whether I'd manage to reach France never mind Africa! Doctors, nurses, receptionists and patients alike proceeded to join me for a run towards Bonchester Bridge. Catching up on the Hawick gossip was terrific. I was back in the real world, and although names and places had changed, the banter had not.

Hawick will forever be associated with rugby, and the noble Bill McLaren. He was the voice of rugby from 1953 until his retirement in 2002, with a turn of phrase almost as impressive as his meticulous preparations. He was a fascinating man, and was on the verge of a Scotland call-up as a player until he developed tuberculosis. As a doctor, the tale of his 19 months in hospital, and revolutionary life saving treatment is intriguing. He began his broadcasting career commentating on table tennis matches in the hospital. Famous quotes attributed to McLaren include "a day out of Hawick is a day wasted," and "he's all arms and legs like a mad octopus," describing Irish winger Simon Geoghegan. We found ourselves indulging in a game of Bill McLaren commentary, with doctors Morrison and Archbold showing a turn of pace "like a trout up a burn," with the warm pub in sight. I was wrecked, feeling as though I'd been tackled by Jonah Lomu. A fantastic couple of days had followed my exam, and huge amounts had been raised for the Yamaa Trust, but I desperately needed a sleep.

Jennie came to join me for a couple days. She is a truly amazing lady. Patient, caring and funny, a couple of stolen days together with Jennie would have me fighting fit for England. The stretch from Bonchester Bridge to the border brought miles of rolling hills, until we crossed into Northumberland near the cheerfully named Deadwater. We were in England. I'd completed a country. One down, four to go. This sense of achievement was dampened not only by the drizzle, but by the fact that everything was still the same. This is far from a bad thing, but the excitement of crossing into a land where cultures or language are different is undoubtedly greater. During breaks and at the end of the day we did some wedding planning. Everything was moving so fast challenge and wedding-wise, and Jennie, although looking calm, had a lot to deal with. For me it was simpler. This was the only day poor weather cheered me up. Surely this gave Scotland a better chance in the rugby against South Africa. So it proved as Scotland produced a performance far more barnstorming than my day's running through the Kielder Forest. The locals in the pub were curious what a drenched and slightly malodorous Scotsman was doing in Bellingham, but enthusiastically offered donations, and the prospect of a shower. Sweeter smells emanated from the campervan. Jennie had produced chorizo pasta as we considered a table plan for our wedding.

84 mile training run on Hadrian's wall with Donnie and Mark Cooper

Winter conditions in England. Photo – Richard Else

Following Day Thirteen's 33 miles, Day Fourteen produced another 33 over hill and down dale, ending up in Rowley. Autumn colours were gradually fading from the trees, and the colder temperatures told me winter was imminent.

Jennie had to get back to work and I wouldn't see her until the south of France. I knew she wished she could accompany and look after me for the whole trip, but work commitments made this impossible. She had a new job as a clinical geneticist, and I was proud this was going so well for her. With heavy hearts, we said our goodbyes, as she went north and I headed south. I felt selfish, literally running away from her at this time, and although Jennie and I have often spent large portions of time away travelling, often independent of each other, it seemed strange being apart for what would be more than a month. She had friends and family that she could talk to, and we'd speak frequently on the phone, but I wasn't tangibly there for her. This was one of my regrets during the expedition, and maybe one I should have considered more thoroughly prior to setting off, but at least it did ensure the time we did spend together was cherished.

CHAPTER 8

Rowley to Scotch Corner and the Gobi Challenge

"I've always wanted to go to Grimsby"

While surveying an atlas my brother Iain had volunteered himself to man the support vehicle for a week. "I've always wanted to go to Grimsby," he joked. He would have a decent chance to fulfil his stated ambition this next week, and he could hardly contain his glee as he trudged through the rain with his fiancée Katie.

"Luke Donald has a brother who carries his golf clubs round Augusta National," he snorted, "I'm watching you run past Scotch Corner in the rain, from a campervan."

What Scotch Corner lacks in beauty, it compensates for in service stations. Doughnuts and coffee galore were swiftly dispatched at the end of a soggy day. Katie, who had joined me for a jog agreed we were living the dream. Iain wasn't so sure.

"How can you do this Andrew? It's so boring. And the weather's terrible. And the roads are rubbish. Why don't you like golf, or at least run in the summer like normal people?" he enquired.

I knew he was part-way joking, but on days like this he had a point. It was actually a bit of a relief having someone pointing out the blatantly obvious, and it took someone such as Iain, who knew he wouldn't actually offend my feelings, to do it. Since I had started, I think everyone had been afraid to say anything negative about what I was attempting, other than that it sounded like a ridiculously hard thing to do.

Iain knew he could get away with giving me pelters on a day when running was almost comically unappealing.

Bizarrely I was reminded of Mongolia. While the climactic conditions were a million miles from Mongolia, and while we were physically 4500 miles from its capital Ulan Bator (as the crow flies), the friendly jibes directed at me were almost identical to those shouted at me by my university friend Duncan Goodall over there.

Mongolia is a land of extremes, and the Gobi Challenge as a race must rank as one of the richest cultural experiences on earth. It is the single race that I have been most excited about participating in prior to going; such were the rave reviews from previous competitors. Outer Mongolia has forever held a sense of awe and mystery for me, and the chance to follow in the hoof prints of Genghis Khan's horses would offer much more besides the 135 mile race.

My perception of Genghis Khan had been as a powerful military leader and a merciless tyrant. The historian William Bonner estimates that as many as 40 million people were killed during his military campaigns, which saw the founding of the Mongolian empire. Upon his death he controlled much of China and indeed Asia. In Mongolia itself, Genghis Khan is much revered as a leader and the nation's founder. He remained a nomad until his death, declaring "perhaps my children will live in stone houses and walled towns – not I."

The sense of space is total. Mongolia is the 19th largest country in the world, and the 146th most populated, giving it one of the lowest population densities in the world. It also suffers great health inequalities, with care for the nomadic herders much poorer than for the increasing urban population. 40% of the population live in Ulan Bator. I'd heard much of the Yamaa Trust's work in addressing unmet needs in the Gobi Desert, through Dave Scott, the race's founder. Having spent eight years directing the Gobi Challenge, and annually spending time living in felt tents with the nomads, Dave along with Phil Briggs had established the Yamaa Trust to input directly where it was most needed.

While also being a race, the Gobi Challenge was more about the imposing sand dunes, towering mountains and seemingly endless sun-baked desert plains to me.

Bill Heirs approaching Asia's largest sand dunes. Photo – Sandbaggers

Looking back on a sea of sand. Photo – Sandbaggers

In this land of extremes, bears, vultures, and wolves as well as nomadic goat herders compete for the few resources available. It is one of the most breathtaking, but least forgiving, places on earth, with temperatures of -30 to -40c in the winter, and plus 30-40c during the short summer. Ulan Bator has the lowest average temperature of any capital city on earth, and the Gobi often sees little rain from one year to the next.

I'd flown in with Duncan via Moscow. The Russians, as I'd previously discovered, appeared to have an almost pathological mistrust of everything and everyone. Unfriendly doesn't do justice to the customs officials who studied each passport in excruciating detail before grunting an approval. We spotted Richard Dunwoody, the legendary jockey, fresh from a trip to the South Pole. He listened attentively as

I bored him with my tales of the two sweepstakes I had won, thanks to his Grand National successes on West Tip, and Minnehoma. More importantly, I immersed myself in more books about Mongolia, and felt I knew a good bit about Genghis Khan by the time we arrived.

The start was in the South Gobi region, next to the South Gobi museum. Although small by British standards, this room gave a flavour of the terrain and topography we would encounter. I helped Duncan set up the medical kit, and check medical forms, before retreating into my tent. I always get both excited and apprehensive before races. I don't usually have problems sleeping, but I do go to the toilet rather a lot and feel continuously fidgety. The organisers pride the race as being a genuine and authentic cultural experience, and consequently, always keep the numbers below 50. Everyone knew everyone else before the race started.

Day one of a self-sufficiency stage race is often the toughest. The weight of equipment and food carried is at its heaviest, and as races often take place in extreme environments, acclimatisation to local conditions is almost non-existent. Some competitors arrive well in advance to acclimatise, or train in a hot gym, with several layers of clothing to simulate the heat. Temperatures of 35 degrees, and ascents up to passes at an altitude of over 2000 metres meant relatively slow progress, which allowed me to appreciate the wild ice gorges carved into the mountains, slicing their ancient paths towards the desert. Evidently everyone else was similarly enchanted, and despite a couple of tumbles, I reached camp in first place. The mental strain of competing in these conditions was equally as overbearing as the sun, and I'd forced myself to count a hundred steps and then repeat this for the last five kilometres. At the finish I found some shade under the ancient Russian vehicles commandeered for the race.

It is virtually impossible to underestimate how demanding a task it is to run in conditions that the body is not accustomed to. The morning of Day 2 broke, and it struck me that it must be an easy job being a weather forecaster in the Gobi desert during the summer. It will be "very hot, very sunny, and there may be occasional clouds later on." I'd set what I thought to be a quick pace, using the cool of the morning to get some quick miles in before the heat kicked in, but the pace seemed like a walk in a very sandy park for a local dog that accompanied me for the first 25 kilometres. I'd already drunk 3.5 litres and had my concerns about the hydration strategies of the dog before we reached water in an ice gorge. Ken the dog had evidently had enough of me and rolled around luxuriously in the stream.

The current guidance from the International Marathon Medical Directors Association, of which I am a member, advises essentially to "drink to thirst." The debate has raged for years as to how to optimally drink during long endurance races, with one camp (including the drinks manufacturers) arguing that even the slightest dehydration causes poor performance, and can be dangerous, while others (including myself, and most race doctors) argue that drinking to thirst may be most appropriate, and that if substantial amounts of salt loss in sweat occurs, it is important to replace these electrolyte losses. Indeed over-drinking with water, without replacing electrolytes, can lead to life threatening hyponatraemia, or low sodium levels.

There is also clear and well-researched objective evidence that eating or drinking carbohydrates during prolonged exercise significantly improves athletic performance. Carbohydrate is the body's preferred fuel, and when this fuel is exhausted, it has to use either fat stores or protein to keep moving. Neither of these are as efficient as using carbohydrate, and if forced to use protein, this involves the body breaking down muscles which further impairs performance. This science explains the 'pasta parties' and carbohydrate loading strategies that runners use prior to a long run. Despite this, it is only possible for the body to store a finite amount of carbohydrate, and when this is finished, it either needs to be replaced or less efficient fuel sources must be used. Runners are generally advised to eat carbohydrate-based snacks regularly during runs, and to eat plenty afterwards to replenish stocks. This is the conundrum that runners face during a self-sufficiency race in which each day's run is a distance of about a standard marathon. The body will perform better if carbohydrate stores are replaced, but to do this would means carrying a huge amount of food, and consequently a heavy backpack.

I'd learnt my lesson and my nutrition strategy involved eating only carbohydrate rich foods before and during each day's run – this was usually a mixture of carbohydrate powder, gels, dried fruit, pop tarts and jelly babies and eating a 4:1 carbohydrate to protein ratio at the finish each day. This allows refuelling of the body with carbohydrate, and allows recovery and repair of the muscles with protein. Nutritionists often describe a 'golden hour' immediately after the finish, when replenishing losses is the most effective. Post run snacks often consist of a commercial pre-prepared drink such as REGO, and could also include noodles with chicken, or rice with dried beef with some chilli flakes thrown in to make it taste slightly less revolting. Current thinking is that the body's fat stores are sufficient to complete all but the very longest of races. My body fat percentage was 8% going into the Gobi race, which gave me enough to get me through the race without eating any extraneous fat. Fatty foods often taste better, so many runners eat them for this reason, but I try to keep the fat content of my food to a minimum.

Ken the dog completed Day 2 accompanying one of the English lads over the finish line. He ate whatever he could get his paws on, and then went for a sleep. As he was clearly a dog of experience, most decided to follow his lead. Applause and a great deal of back-slapping greeted each runner as they made the finish and helping out with the medical team well illustrated the kind of troubles some were experiencing. Brian Jenkins was already missing a couple of toenails, and had a blister that almost engulfed his whole foot. He'd spent the day running on raw skin, and had tried everything blister treatment-wise.

The route from Bayan Bag to Tohum Bag started well. I had company initially with David "Fitzy" Fitzgerald, and we set off briskly, running the first 11km in 52 minutes. While this might not sound brisk, the sand and the heat forced the field to string out behind us. Reminiscent of Iain, Duncan had found the confidence to offer simultaneous words of abuse and encouragement, and kept me entertained throughout the week, pointing out how comfortable his air conditioned car was, and that the food he was eating was a fair bit more appetising than mine. Fitzy works as a fireman, but complained that he'd never felt heat like this.

He was a great example of the courage and singularity of purpose by which ultra runners are often characterised. He'd slowed, and was eventually forced to rest for an hour in a medical car, suffering from heat related symptoms. He'd worked out a strategy with Duncan to get him to the finish which included going a fair bit slower, eating plenty of carbohydrate, and buddying up with other runners. Duncan showed the qualities he always does at races. A doctor with a cool head, a recognition of the importance of the challenge to the runner, and knowledge of how to get runners to the finish safely. Fitzy reached the Tohum Bag with my good friend Alan Silcock, still looking extremely shaky. Alan had had his own problems. He'd complained of profound fatigue throughout the day. Further probing revealed that Alan, usually the master of having his kit in order, had inadvertently taken several sleeping tablets instead of painkillers. I doubt I'll ever let him forget this, but he did sleep soundly that evening.

The finish in the Oasis of Tahum Bag was Mongolia as the postcards portray it. We sheltered in a nomad village, with blue mountains on each side, and very little else. Medical facilities for the collapsed runners at the finish were rudimentary, with the ever smiling Mongolian doctors explaining a little of Mongolia and its medicine to us, and Duncan and myself reciprocating between taking temperatures, blood pressures, and dishing out treatments. The local doctors seemed to have a bewildering array of unusual sounding remedies that made me think that being a doctor would be more enjoyable here than back home. Interacting in this way, and having the chance to work out and help with Yamaa Trust projects made this a memorable and busy week. The nomadic way of life is very simple, and very little seems to grow, so the cheese and goat meat diet eaten by the locals is typical of the area. Cardiovascular disease accounts for about 30% of deaths in Mongolia, and the diet almost appeared Scottish but without the sugar. A dentist had volunteered as part of the Yamaa Trust a previous year, and had claimed never to have seen such good teeth despite a lack of brushing. The Mongolian doctors asked me a couple times if I could remove teeth – clearly the legend of the white dentist had spread – although this was well beyond my scope of practice.

*(Top) The author's tiny figure in Mongolia's expanse. (bottom left) A local nomad. (bottom right) A well earned finishers' medal.
Photos – Sandbaggers*

The hospitality of the locals was genuine, and unstinting. The experience seemed unusually authentic, perhaps due to the deliberate restriction of numbers. The fourth day featured a long climb into the mountains for the finish. It would have been an unbeatable place to go rock climbing, but all I could think of was ticking off each checkpoint, collecting a bottle of water at each, putting my head down, and reaching the finish. Despite the grandeur of the mountains there are days that for no reason I get lost in a negative spiral of thoughts, and all I wanted was to be finished. Day 5 was very different. The biggest sand dunes in Asia formed the horizon, and following a literal and metaphorical warm up on the plains, it was up into the dunes. Most races will stagger the start after a few days, allowing the quicker runners to start later. Almost everyone loves this, and I relished the support and banter of the earlier runners we passed. The dunes, with the mountains behind them, were unforgettable. Route selection is the key to success, and I followed the advice of nine times Marathon des Sables champion Lahcen Ahansal, who had told me on a previous trip to the desert to try the dunes with the shallowest slopes and the most footsteps, adding, "sometimes you don't know, sometimes we are wrong."

Reassured that even the greatest of all desert racers finds the dunes a challenge, I huffed and puffed my way to the finish. The dunes are beguiling, and were very much my master. The last day, in the biggest dunes in Asia is without doubt the most incredible day's desert scenery I have witnessed. The early starters moved like ants up the faces of these beasts, and seemed equally as awestruck as I. Seeing others pushing themselves, and being honest, seeing others struggling just as badly often steels me into trying harder, and with this being the last day, everyone was on full throttle. Almost vertical dunes acted to carry me backwards and my legs stung with unbearable cramps. Pausing wasn't an option as this would have ensured further movement backwards, and following a battle mostly with my own mind I toiled finally onto the sand ridge. The sands were singing as the winds reverberated through them. China lay to my left, Mongolia stretched endlessly on my right. Superlatives are overused, but the journey along the ridge, and the sprint down from the dunes to camp, were unbelievable. To run here from

Scotland would be amazing I thought. I'd finished first overall, and broken the course record, but that was nothing compared to the runners who had battled injuries and ailments all week. Having been in their shoes before, I knew keeping injury free had made things ten times easier.

Sitting in the sandy amphitheatre of camp, watching others on the dunes was surreal. The goat curd and meat produced by the nomads on a stove fuelled by camel and goat dung at the finish tasted like manna from heaven. This formidable and unyielding land had it all for a tourist, but offered less to the inhabitants. With the locals enormously appreciative of any help we could offer, I vowed to join Dave and Phil in an effort to improve the standard of living in the Gobi. Witnessing the work already done, and meeting those our work would directly benefit, made me twice as determined. Perhaps more unusually, Aberdeen FC has an unwitting supporter's base in the Gobi. Duncan and I had dished out a load of replica tops that we had collected.

Iain had donated his old Aberdeen tops to the people of Mongolia. "Do they know about football in Mongolia, "he asked me. "What do they think about you running about in the desert."

I assured him that although archery and wrestling were the main sports in Mongolia, Aberdeen could not wish for a more loyal support. "They'll wear the tops every day this year."

CHAPTER 9
Scotch Corner to London

"Pain is transient, memories are forever."

With Katie heading back to Northern Ireland to plan her and Iain's wedding, we headed inexorably south towards Tollerton, another 34 miles distant. Anyone planning to repeat this route will have the opportunity to pass through Bolton-On-Swale and Airenby Steeple prior to the "World of James Herriot" (the legendary vet), which is in Thirsk. These small roads and towns made for pleasant running before the busy A19, where it seemed motorists competed to drown me with the biggest puddle. Towards the end of each day, I was knackered. I'd found that to help the Achilles recover, and to get adequate food on board, I'd take breaks in the campervan fairly regularly before cracking on. Depending on the terrain, I'd usually be relatively OK for the first 25-30 miles, but for the last few miles my energy levels would drop, everything would hurt, and I would mutter dark thoughts under my breath. It was usually at this juncture my feet felt like they had done 12 rounds with a lawnmower. As a rule, the more I wasn't thinking about anything (other than route selection), the better I was. Often I'd slip into a world of thinking about various injuries I had, or the weather forecast, and have to mentally force myself to think positively, or take my mind off things in other ways. I would have found music useful, but wasn't keen to have headphones on when running on the road. I'd usually leave Iain to make any decisions, as he declared me incapable towards the end of a day. He claimed, probably with Mongolia in mind, that looking after me "was like herding a goat."

A days' running ahead of me. Photo – Susie Lind

He decided that in Tollerton we'd stay in the Angel Inn. In the mid 18th century this route had been tolled, hence the village's name. Travellers paid the toll to buy protection when passing through the forest of Galtres from rapscallions, wild boar, and other unsavoury beasts.

The Angel Inn proved to be a marvellous choice. Checking on the trip advisor website, Iain noticed that every single review had given the Inn 5/5 stars. He bundled me to the door to announce our arrival. Richard the owner looked slightly shocked to see a man in shorts when it was minus three outside and ushered us to our room.

"What type of jam would you like with your scones, gentlemen?" he asked.

Hardly used to this sort of luxury we chomped heartily into the freshly baked scones, served on a Paisley patterned tray, with matching Paisley napkins, by the proprietor dressed in a Paisley apron. We decided to treat ourselves to dinner too, in the local pub. This was less delightful as we endured some thoroughly dreadful cuisine while dodging darts thrown errantly by the local team. I watched in horror as one chap in particular belched and drank his way through the evening, while devouring countless bags of peanuts and portions of chips. He was quite the potty-mouth, having colourful language for things as inanimate as a bar stool, and a bag of peanuts. I didn't have the heart to complain about my soup, which had probably been strained through a sock, the chicken dips which were still partially frozen, and a pizza I doubt a seagull would eat. Back in the utopia of the Angel Inn, breakfast was predictably excellent. Everything was homemade, the service was impeccable and it was a wrench to drag myself out and onto the road to York, and past the scene of the previous night's culinary crimes.

The city of York is apparently built on the terminal moraine left by the last ice age, and boasts some wonderful sights. Iain ran with me, with the handycam bobbing in and out of the tourists at the city walls and York Minster. I was absolutely desperate for a pee and sped up, frantically searching for a McDonald's or similar. I'm sure most runners can identify with this, and it must be worse for ladies I guess. I ran enviously past a dog relieving itself on a wall, and eventually came up trumps in a cafe which also stocked Irn Bru. Result! It's funny how the simplest things could cheer me up. I'd tried hard to avoid busy roads, but the A19 south would save some time. Arriving onto it, I saw a "no pedestrians, cycles, or horse drawn carts" sign. Being honest, I didn't much like the look of three lanes of traffic and no hard shoulder, so a frustrating back track took me on the B1222 towards Naburn instead.

Speaking to a local, Naburn is apparently famous for having been the site of the York Psychiatric hospital. It is presently the home of Naburn sewage treatment centre. Even at my least fragrant after four days with no shower, I doubt I was a match for Naburn. Snow began to fall, with just enough to make the numerous power plants on the road to Snaith more pretty. The smog clouds contributed to a glorious sunset. At the end of this day, I was so impressed by the scale of the sewage plant that I researched it more thoroughly. According to local journalist Charlotte Percival, writing in a local paper, "Waste water that would fill around 43 Olympic swimming pools is pumped into York's sewerage treatment works in Naburn each day, with thousands of litres arriving each second."

Further research revealed that tomato plants are often found in sewage plants, as the human body cannot digest the seeds, and cannabis plants are also frequently found, presumably after it is flushed down the toilet in haste! I declined any tomato based dish for dinner, fearing that they may be well nourished local produce.

I had settled into running 34 miles every day. My Achilles tendons had improved but were still troublesome. Iain was threatening a world of mischief, as plans for my stag party fell into place. The current plan was to finish bang on Day 85, arriving back on the Friday of the stag do, the weekend before our wedding. A thimbleful of beer could be enough to cause mayhem! The thought of it cheered me as the scenery now was less inspiring than up north and for the first time I was becoming a bit bored when I was running. I started to count the tractors we passed. The next day's run to Treswell was broken up by the visit of Dan Broadhead, a highly regarded podiatrist with Patterson Medical, who had offered to come out and assess my gait and biomechanics while on the road. This is an extract from his report.

"Meeting on a pavement, in freezing temperatures, is not the ideal initial appointment with a patient, however this was no ordinary patient! Andrew presented with blisters between the toes, callus on both feet and more importantly a swollen and painful Achilles tendon. Both Achilles tendons had been problematic throughout the run.

"We began the assessment with a static weight bearing, then non-weight bearing analyses of Andrew's feet. Nothing glaringly wrong. I then assessed Andrew jogging at his perceived average pace – Andrew was running on a pavement that had inclines, declines, pot holes, may even have been on a camber and all after running a total of 500 to 600 miles before this assessment. Andrew had very good foot function, however there was quite a large amount of movement/oscillation at the rear foot when he ran. This seems to possibly be leading to an overuse injury in the Achilles tendon. I feel for a recreational runner and even a marathon runner this problem would not have lead to an overuse injury but due to the colossal number of miles Andrew was running the Achilles never had time to recover. The varying cambers at the side of the road which could create an artificial limb length discrepancy, are probably contributing to his injury.

"With this in mind and the assessment we carried out, I advised Andrew to rest and ice the Achilles to allow it to recover and to also seek the treatment of a physiotherapist, but clearly this was not going to happen as Andrew was committed to his challenge

"As Andrew's injury was determined to be due to overuse and his foot posture was very good we decided controlling the speed and amplitude of the pronation and supination movements would be the best course of action. Thankfully Formthotics were the perfect option so we could provide control, stability and support for Andrew."

Dan felt there was a tiny imbalance that had contributed to my Achilles problems and suggested I wear an orthotic, and sorted me out for heel raises, ice packs, blister treatments etc. The generosity of Dan and others astounded me. To wade through the snow to treat a Scottish lunatic he had heard of through a friend was a great example of the kindness and consistent support I encountered from strangers.

Looking forward to a hot chocolate. Photo – Richard Else

Further brightening my day, I learned of a huge corporate donation from Vivergo Fuels. Seeing these donations flood in, and knowing the impact they would have in Mongolia was unbelievably inspiring, as well as the faith shown in me by these companies. Vivergo were full of ideas on how they could help further, and it was brilliant to hear some of the ideas they had, and how we could utilise their business acumen.

What a great day. People believed, and this fortified my conviction that our goals would be achieved. Vivergo were investing substantially in the project; Dan Broadhead had driven hours and performed a roadside assessment and treatment in sub zero conditions; and Iain was giving up sunnier climes to reside in a campervan in winter for a week. While having adequate physical fitness, preparing correctly, and all the rest of it was important, the knowledge that I was convinced I would reach the Sahara, and that others felt the same way was as important as any of these other factors. Without mental strength, achieving your goals becomes more difficult. Supporters strengthen you with their belief, although listening to Iain singing Susie Boyle songs is enough to make anyone get out the van and run. I'll be buying Katie some headphones for her next birthday!

We stayed at the Canal View Bed and Breakfast near Lincoln. The welcome, and attention to detail was phenomenal. I was in the habit of checking the fundraising total whenever I could, and before I went to bed I noticed a very generous donation from Roland and the Canal View team. My feet felt like glass, after a day skidding around on the ice, and a soak in the shower was just what the doctor ordered.

Weather reports stated that there was heaps of snow everywhere. We had largely missed it until now. Whereas the last two days had brought just enough snow to make the scenery look pretty, it now snowed properly. I loved it, although it made running more difficult. It was a novelty, and the scenery in the previous few days had been mundane. Since the terrain had flattened out, I managed 34 or 35 miles per day. On Day 19 I only managed 32.5 miles despite being out there pretty much all day but it was beautiful. I had been in shorts throughout, and this was the first day I was being regularly labelled a 'nutter'. We got some great footage of myself and the van sliding about in the ice, and I was invited in by a local farmer for a warming brandy, which I can commend thoroughly. He told me there were "strong medications for people like you," and bade me farewell with a grin and stern advice to invest in a decent bottle of Cognac.

Webasto had kindly put a heating system into the van, and this was to prove a godsend over the next fortnight. I was also getting through industrial quantities of hot chocolate. Navigating through these cold conditions is a more complex business than it sounds. Usually when I go running, it's either a route I know, or up in the hills with a map and compass. I found it much prettier and less dangerous running on the smaller roads. This often has the bonus of taking you through villages, although this too can be a baffling process. There were very few occasions I got seriously lost, and this was principally due to Iain, and other support drivers, as well as I-Phone GPS systems and the like. This was especially the case this day, with fresh snow obscuring the road signs. The pedestrian was king on days like this, with drivers struggling to get through, and it seemed most were out on sledges. My exams results were supposed to have been issued this day, but had been delayed due to the snow. Whether this, or overeating, led to me vomiting several times I'm not too sure, but the food definitely tasted better the first time.

Grantham, I was informed, was the birthplace of Margaret Thatcher. I am sure she would be horrified by the behaviour of a couple of lads throwing snowballs from a flyover bridge at the traffic. I felt it necessary to go up and discourage them and spent a few seconds chasing them in Benny Hill fashion before deciding my legs were not up to it and retreating to the van to dry off.

Grantham is also notable for producing the first tractor in the UK. This impressed me greatly, and with the outskirts of Peterborough the next day's target, I amused myself by counting tractors again. For a kilometre or two the A1 was virtually unavoidable, and there were no tractors there. I had been dreading this stretch, along one of Britain's busiest roads, but there was a handy cycle path. Heading south, the volume of snow diminishedand the roads were busier again. The running in the snow had triggered both my knees to hurt, as well as my left Achilles. I must admit, when planning I expected a bit of snow in Scotland when passing over the higher passes, and especially through the High Atlas Mountains of Morocco, and the Pyrenees in Spain, but in England this had initially been a pleasant surprise. It had never been overly deep to run through, six inches in Grantham at the most, but the campervan and my knees were starting not to enjoy it. More snow meant fewer miles and getting back up to 34 miles a day felt good. I had started to feel a little dissatisfied if I ran less than this, unless there was a good reason why I couldn't.

My sister Susie lives in London, and she had offered to support me for a nine-day stretch. She arrived clutching boxes of cakes, an ice pack, and other welcome goodies. Susie is amongst the most enthusiastic and charitable people I know, and she was going to have to be at the peak of her powers. Reading through the messages of support on Facebook and Twitter was another boost. I was getting a fair amount of abuse for my navigating 'skills' but well wishing was at an all time high. It was currently minus nine and very snowy in the north, exactly where Iain was heading for.

A crisp sunrise with a dusting of snow greeted me on Day 21. The road was like a skating rink. The shoes I wore coped better than the cars in temperatures that were still minus nine, and I began to suspect the temperature sensor on the van

My sister Susie Lind, in charge of the camper

SCOTCH CORNER TO LONDON

didn't go below that figure. I was right. The BBC weather forecast said it was actually minus thirteen! In Braemar in the Scottish highlands it was apparently minus twenty six! Regardless of the temperature, it was cold enough for any moisture to freeze instantly, and my legs were swathed in tiny white hairs. I put an extra pair of boxer shorts on to avoid any other unwanted cold injuries. The Fen Tiger, aka Mark Howlett, had volunteered for a Sunday jog. It warmed up considerably to about freezing allowing Mark to discourse on army bases, various runs and other matters to jolly me along. It's not often that I was in this area, and I took the chance to catch up with friends Mark and Alice, who bought us a delicious dinner in a festively decorated hotel.

Day 22 comprised 33.8 miles. It was November 29th, and the snow was minimal just north of London. Susie, and the awesome Jenna and Team Tribesport had arranged for a fun run in London for that night following a day's running. It was certainly a run, and was fun for me if not everyone else. There was a fantastic turnout despite a London Tube strike and temperatures of around freezing. It was probably the group of people least likely to be deterred by a Tube strike. Raffles, food, and cheap beer and Bacardi at the Duck in Clapham junction ensured a great fundraiser and no doubts some sore heads in the morning. There was much hilarity over stories appearing in the papers about my avoidance of wedding preparations, and I had the chance to catch up with Jennie's mum and dad, and assure them I'd be back in time, hopefully fit and healthy.

There were also a multitude of amazing stories being told, of runs and challenges in weird and wonderful locations, including Tobias Mews, who planned to run a marathon every day for 50 days in a different European country each day. It sounded brilliant. "Probably avoid winter, the transport could be a nightmare," was the only sensible advice I could offer.

These were fun times, and although having a large amount of things going on probably cuts the distance you can do on a given day, it's brilliant for morale, and fundraising. This certainly applied to Day 23. Steve and Arnaud from Team Tribesport jogged into Central London with me. Arnaud had never run a marathon before, and had already ran six miles to the start. What a legend.

They guided me past Buckingham Palace (no sign of the Queen) and down to the houses of Parliament. A great bit of advice I'd been given by the endurance cyclist Mark Beaumont was to break the challenge down into bite sized chunks, rather than having the weight of the entire distance looming over me. This can make distant targets seem more achievable. Each day I'd knock off 10km chunks in my mind until the day was done, and each week there were targets. Arriving at Parliament was one such landmark.

Big Ben's chimes were drowned out by a raucous student protest over fees. We'd arrived a bit early for our planned run with some MP's. University friend and parliamentary aid Alan Gillam had persuaded 10-20 MP's to bring in their running kit and brave the snow that was falling. The Mongolian Ambassador had been alerted to the run and fundraising for the South Gobi region of his country, and he made some kind comments over a coffee. It is not every day you sit down to coffee with HE Bulgaa Altangerel, the Mongolian Ambassador, and I regretted forgetting the Ferrero Rocher I had planned to offer His Excellency. Both he, and his first secretary, showed a keen interest in all things Scottish, particularly the whisky industry. Dave Scott had flown down as founder of the Yamaa Trust and we were escorted through the historic Westminster Hall. I'm not certain if the Westminster dress code approves of shorts, a high-viz jacket and squelchy shoes, but no-one commented. No doubt to some relief from a few MP's, due to the student protests, there would be a photo shoot inside rather than a run. My local MP, Ian Murray, seemed genuinely disappointed about the run's cancellation. Alan said that Ian had been as keen as mustard despite the inclement conditions. Myself, the Ambassadorial staff and Dave were received with great enthusiasm, and all seemed keen on my twin agendas of the importance of exercise and the amelioration of poverty in Mongolia. Early day motions (EDM's) to increase the awareness of these issues have been actioned, and Ian Murray, and his colleagues' sincerity in recognising and promoting these matters continues to be exceedingly helpful. Another agenda was to warm up, and we did so in the parliamentary bar which must serve the cheapest booze in central London.

CHAPTER 10

The 6633 Arctic Ultra

*"Conditions had improved.
It was minus 44 degrees celcius."*

For the second night we stayed at Susie's house in Clapham Junction. Susie had recently married Graham, and it was brilliant to see them so happy. Appropriately, given the chilly conditions, my friend Chris Todd and his wife Joy came to join us. Chris is a terrific runner, with his races including two wins in the 350 mile-long 6633ultra, which is dubbed as the hardest race in the world. I'd competed in the shorter 120 mile version in 2009, and provided medical cover for the longer version. Many races claim to be the hardest. I can only speak for the ones I have raced or worked at but the unremittingly severe weather gives my vote to the 6633ultra so far. Chris had brought his racing sledge, which I would require when support was more spread out later on. It is much easier to pull a sledge than carry a large amount of weight on your back. Chris is an inventor as well as an engineer. This is a happy combination for sledge making, and I was delighted to borrow his, having shredded my own in Canada. Seeing Chris was good for morale. Although he didn't say it, speaking to him reminded that me whatever this challenge threw at me, the conditions would never deteriorate to the level of the 6633ultra, where we'd run our respective races despite temperatures of minus 50 and minus 80 including windchill. I remembered those days and shivered. Compared to that the snow here was perfectly manageable.

The 6633ultra had gained esteem and notoriety amongst ultra runners as the coldest, wildest and windiest race out there. I have yet to meet a runner who has taken the course on, and not claimed it to be both an amazing and epic event. Reading reports from previous years told me this was to be a true Arctic experience. I think there is, inherent in most people, an impulse that tells them to push their limits, and to embrace challenges, whether this is at work, or at leisure. I'd been mesmerised by the grandeur and majesty of the Arctic when I was working and running at the geographical North Pole, and couldn't resist the temptation of providing medical expertise for the 350 mile race, and running the 120 miler.

Being honest, the prospect of looking after competitors worried me more than the run itself, and a great deal of time was invested in constructing risk assessments and planning. The races take place almost entirely within the Arctic Circle in early to mid March, and this necessitates unusual precautions with the medical kit, where the most common injury would almost certainly be frostbite. This inescapable fact was rammed home as we congregated in Dawson city, centre of the Klondike Gold Rush. Kit checks, safety briefs, medical assessments and a drive up the Dempster Highway had left everyone weary, so we headed for the bar. The Canadian sub-Arctic has always been cold, and with supplies having to be hauled by sled in the winter initially, frostbite was an occupational hazard for the workers. One severed toe was preserved in alcohol, until the idea came to celebrate this with a cocktail. Thus the 'Sourtoe Cocktail' is tried by many, and enjoyed by few. I count myself in the former camp only. Apparently there have had to be several replacements for the original toe, due to overzealous drinkers. House rules state, "You can drink it fast, you can drink it slow, but your lips have got to touch the toe."

The start line for the race was at Eagle Plains, actually 23 miles south of the Arctic Circle, before heading due north. There were three events, a standard marathon, a 120-mile race, and the 350-miler. The atmosphere was more akin to a climbing expedition than a race, with everyone lending each other kit and advice. All the runners had been vetted and were highly experienced. The race was to be completely self sufficient, save for shelter every 30-40 miles or so. We'd haul our gear on polar pulks, with a metal bar attaching the sledge to ourselves. I actually had most of the bomb proof cold weather gear from climbing trips to Alaska but had borrowed a sledge from the ever helpful race organisers Martin and Sue Like.

Heading up towards the mountains and Wright Pass. Photo – Martin Like

Word spread that the start may be delayed, high winds of 80mph had closed the road at Hurricane Alley, and support vehicles to set up the checkpoints could not get through. I'm not a builder, but to paraphrase Bill McLaren, I was laying bricks that night.

Conditions had improved overnight and the race would start on time. It was minus 44 Celcius, according to the thermometer, and much colder still in the buffeting wind. Three of the support crew had considered running the standard marathon distance, but this was vetoed due to the severity of the weather. Medical coverage was full on, with two medics and two first aiders available to care for the nine runners, not including myself. Medically, the competitors were equipped for these conditions and we were happy to let the race proceed. My feet were literally freezing, as wearing full climbing boots would be impractical to run in, so I'd plumped for Gore-Tex trainers several sizes too large, with feet warmers and three pairs of thick socks. The gun went and I shot off like Meatloaf's Bat out of Hell just to warm up. I remembered checking the stats prior to entering, and being astonished that only about 33% of runners finish the 120-mile race, and less than 20% the 350-miler. Surely it can't be that hard I thought?

The reality of the situation bit. I'd blasted off the front purely to get warm, and had started to sweat. When this froze, as would be inevitable, having ice next to the skin would be game over. I opened a few vents in my jackets, and took one off. Mountains enclosed us, but the wind whipped round from every direction. Immediately after the support vehicle drove past to tell me it had dropped to minus 50 Celcius, my sledge broke. This was my own fault. I'd tested it, but not properly with all the supplies weighing it down, and subject to the wrath of the Arctic. One of the poles had snapped a bracket off, leaving it skewing from my harness. Knowing Chris to be an aeronautical engineer, I'd taken some tips on maintenance from him prior to the race. Using a spanner while wearing mitts is impossible, and I stripped to two base layers of gloves to sort the problem. The fix wasn't ideal, but sufficed. I'd frost nipped my fingers before and knew that working with little hand protection and metal parts had already led to some tissue damage.

I crested a summit to view an expanse of the most inhospitable, but stunning scenery the planet has to offer. Mountains rose and fell. I was at 712 metres, beyond the Arctic Circle, and at the finish of the marathon. More importantly this was one of only three checkpoints, and I could fix my sledge properly. There are no houses between the truck stop at the start and Fort McPherson at the finish. Huddling in the back of a vehicle felt like the Ritz hotel, and I forced about 3000 calories down, and repaired the sledge.

The world was white as I entered what is affectionately known as Hurricane Alley. The valley follows seemingly endless peaks and troughs, which mirrored my temperament. Every mouthful of food was a mission – you had to hold it close enough to the skin to thaw before eating it. This wasn't so much a race, but pure survival. The many hills were icy enough that microspikes (like small crampons) would have been useful, especially as the sledge dragged me backwards at such times.

Another competitor slogging up towards Wright Pass. Photo – Martin Like

Magnificent but harsh conditions. Photo – Martin Like

THE 6633 ARCTIC ULTRA

I speeded up aiming for Rock River, the checkpoint at 85km at the foot of Wright Pass. Its bulk lay before me, the road shimmering in the pitch dark.

Wright Pass is correctly considered the most brutal section of the course. A long uphill slogged across a mountain, completely exposed to the elements. I had two balaclavas, which I wore closest to my skin alternately, to allow the frozen vapour from my breathing to melt slightly. It was as cold as it had been at its worst climbing Mount McKinley/ Denali, which is known as one of the coldest mountains on earth, but I remember thinking we wouldn't have climbed Denali with this wind speed. At the dead of night, with the wind howling, warmth was impossible, and I ran as quickly as I had done at any point during the run. Martin had parked beyond the top, to check I'd made it OK, and was in a frenzy in his truck. "Great stuff Andrew, what do you think of the light show."

Having been hidden by the mountain, the Northern Lights danced into view. Mad yellows, and sheets of sulphurous green rippled heavenward. There are no words that could do this justice but I'd miscalculated on the balaclava front. I'd been breathing so heavily pushing up the hill that the mask had frozen solid to my face. I yanked it off, pulling a little skin and plenty of my beard off and swapped balaclavas over. I ran inexorably towards the Aurora, drawn like a moth towards the lights.

James Creek offered some respite. At 70 miles it was the last checkpoint, and I tried to sleep, with minimal success, for four hours. Essentially it was a highways agency depot, with snow clearance vehicles roaring around constantly. No-one else had followed me over Wright Pass, probably wisely waiting for a little daylight. Hauling a sledge while running is a vastly different discipline than running without, and I developed injuries I'd never had before. Not even dragging a tyre can prepare you for it. My hip flexors screamed blue murder, and my shins were very painful.

Still there was only 50 miles to go, and none of it could be as bad as Wright Pass. I spotted a pair of Arctic foxes, and was happier that now I was out of the more major hills conditions were better.

Northern Lights at Inuvik

It is amazing the difference that minus 30 Celcius makes compared to minus 40. It felt positively balmy running towards Fort McPherson. My injuries had deteriorated, forcing me to walk sections of the route. I spent several pit stops repairing my sledge, resorting eventually to the universal tool of Gaffer Tape, a last minute addition to the sledge on the advice of the well informed organisers. I felt a click in my left shin and I suddenly felt uncontrollably nauseus, vomiting next to the sledge. I was sure I'd stress fractured my tibia and looked around for a support vehicle. The Mackenzie delta shimmered below in the evening light. This was when being on the ice was an advantage. Although it was still mighty sore, sliding my left foot along the ice was infinitely preferable to having to strike the ground with it. Running with a fracture in the main bone supporting my lower leg remains easily the most painful experience of my life, but I finally crawled into MacPherson accompanied by some enthusiastic locals on skidoos.

I punched the air as one of the most tortuous, but incredible of runs came to an end for me.

Providing medical cover, while actually partaking in a race, is not really compatible. I'd had no medical involvement up until then other than in the planning, but would assist the team for the 350 mile race, as runners would be scattered many miles apart. I looked in the mirror to assess my own injuries, and confirmed frost nip of both cheeks and of several fingers. Exquisite pain in one particular spot virtually confirmed a stress fracture, but I was otherwise well. Of the nine starters, three had already pulled out with frost nip, shin, and back injuries, and were safe. The other runners were strung out 30-60 miles behind. I slept, having offered to relieve the medics after I'd slept. They had done a superb job checking and treating patients in the severest of weather.

During the night Ed Chapman, a hugely experienced ultra runner, and a man who had prepared systematically, was brought in to McPherson. A first aider had picked him up on Wright Pass. From a very accurate description he'd clearly been hypothermic, and spotted in the nick of time. The wind chill temperature was minus 75 Celcius and he was wobbling. For a man as gnarly and tough as Edward to succumb to the conditions proved the magnitude of the test. He was in remarkable spirit as we assessed and treated the frostbite he had sustained to his thigh, lower leg and face. It further vindicated the organiser's attention to detail, and the placement of experienced staff on this dangerous stretch.

News came through that all had crossed Wright Pass, and Chris Todd and Doug Girling arrived safely in McPherson. Chris was leading the 350 mile race by about 24 hours, and Doug was second to myself in the 120 miler. Both demonstrated ingenuity in the systems they had dreamed up to combat the forces of winter. They had both constructed breathing pipes to avoid the problem of their facemasks freezing, which made them look like deep-sea divers running in the Arctic, but which functioned perfectly. Doug had substantial frost nip to his fingers and a little on his face, while Chris still looked pretty. This guy clearly knew what he was doing; he hadn't broken his sledge, or his leg, and continued his serene passage north after a sleep. I love watching someone performing a task well, and effortlessly in life, whatever it is. Watching Chris advance to Inuvik, and finally onto the famous Mackenzie River ice road was like seeing Roger Federer play tennis, or a surgeon perform an operation. He was precise, unflustered, and in almost complete and embarrassing contrast to me. He was the only finisher to reach the igloo in the Arctic Ocean that signified the finish of the 350 mile race in 2009. Phillip Howells, a courageous and gregarious Welshman, showed a great deal of resilience before becoming another victim of hypothermia in what were extreme conditions.

Speaking with Martin Like, he describes the 6633ultra as an experience, rather than necessarily a race. Certainly there is far more to it that just the event, and further viewings of the Northern Lights, husky racing, and various other Arctic pursuits were available. He also regaled us with stories of interesting characters that had preceeded my trip including Mimi Anderson. Mimi has a reputation of taking on the hardest of challenges and succeeding. She still holds the course record, male or female, for the 350 mile race. This she accomplished, despite hallucinating regularly due to a lack of sleep and horrific conditions. She describes seeing, "an elephant, hundreds of men on skidoos about to attack me, men carrying guns standing near parked cars – I even closed my eyes and counted to ten knowing that none of this was real, on opening my eyes they were still there and had not moved!"

These perceptions, in the absence of an external stimuli (which defines a hallucination) are often described in athletes who are sleep deprived. I've never actually hallucinated myself, but interviews conducted with athletes show this to be not uncommon. The tenacity of Mimi, and Chris's supreme control of the situation illustrated my limitations as a runner.

Hauling the sledge after running repairs. Photo – Martin Like

CHAPTER 11

London to Le Mans

"Go confidently in the direction of your dreams."

HENRY THOREAU

This object lesson struck me, as back in London Chris pointed many things about the route and the van that were perfectly obvious when he pointed them out, but that hadn't occurred to me. Having his sledge, which had been crafted like a Picasso, rather than anything cobbled together by myself, for any time where hauling in the desert would be required was a great bonus. He wished me well, while using words to describe pieces of a sledge that are usually reserved for heavy and incomprehensible books.

Day 24 and 25 featured the race south to make the ferry at Newhaven. I had envisaged having two recovery days of 31 miles each which would set me up nicely for the continent. Gav Brown, Jennie's sister's husband joined me from the previous day's finish point at Westminster. We discussed cricket as we passed the Oval cricket ground. Snow was falling. London had largely escaped the carnage that enveloped southern England but Gatwick airport was the abode of the snow. No flights flew for several days and an ethereal mist hung over it. The occasional train was running, although cars were really struggling. By now the snow fell at a rate usually reserved for cartoons and Christmas cards. Only the main transport arteries were open and Susie would take the main roads in the van and I would take smaller ones and meet up where able. On forays to the main road I pushed at least five cars out of the snow. The pedestrian was king and it was possibly easier to run the 31 miles than drive it that day. The back roads had not been cleared.

A crisp winter's day in France. Photo – Richard Else

I wished I'd brought my snow shoes as I slogged though shin and occasionally knee deep powder. I had these roads to myself and executed a swan dive along the road at one point, before regretting it almost instantly.

As a surprise Jennie had come to London for a conference, and we'd steal a few hours together. I was astonished she'd made it, with transport being as it was. We didn't even have to say anything to each other, but appreciated having this snowy reunion prior to seeing her next in the presumably sunnier Biarritz.

When imagining the route, I'd thought the Newhaven to Dieppe ferry crossing would be ideal. I could visit friends in Brighton, and enjoy a flattish end to Great Britain. In the event, day 25 yielded similar conditions to day 24, although the roads had been ploughed slightly. Richard Else from the Triple Echo crew had managed to get a train from London to East Grinstead. Normally not an act of courage this equated to a great success, and he filmed from the campervan this day.

The weather did mellow towards the coast but I'll never forget running straight down the middle of an almost desolate A22. On the days where heavy snow lay, there was always great enthusiasm. People usually stopped me and asked exactly what I was doing, and would often run a few yards with me. Most seemed to attribute this unusual behaviour to my being Scottish as if this was a prerequisite for eccentric behaviour during freak weather. Perhaps we Scots are a bit more used to snowy weather.

I had a real feeling of achievement when I arrived in Newhaven after a total of 811 miles. We'd made the ferry on time, the fundraising had topped £31000, and most surprising of all, I'd been told that I'd passed the exam. I'd be feasting on pain au chocolat this time tomorrow. Perhaps more impressively, Susie had steered the campervan safely to the ferry. What did surprise me was my school friend Doug Gordon arriving on a bike. He'd cycled the coast road from Brighton. When asked why, he told me the buses and trains had been cancelled due to snow. I'd hoped to catch up with Doug, but this was a hard core act of friendship. As a culinary adieu to Britain, I dispatched double portions of bangers and mash and apple pie and headed for the port.

A mild drama on the high seas hit Team *Scotland2Sahara* as an irregularity with Susie's passport meant she would not be able to cross that night, but would wait until the next day. These administrative frustrations are inevitable, but I was sad I couldn't cross with Susie. She had worked night and day to put on the event in London, keep me fed, and had driven in treacherous conditions. I'd enjoyed spending time with her, as this is usually all too infrequent with her base being in London. Nevertheless we were hopeful she could get the first ferry the next day. Arriving in Dieppe at 0330 felt strange. I wasn't alone, having travelled with Richard and Carrie from Triple Echo. They had become friends, and a comfort, but the streets were empty, and with the campervan yet again reading its favourite minus 9 Celcius I wondered whether we'd taken the ferry to Siberia by accident. I gladly accepted the offer to crash for a few hours in the spare bed in Richard's hotel.

After three hours sleep, I woke and got out the maps. Carrie and Richard agreed on a route that looked pretty but passable, and kindly agreed to drop the van at the day's finish while keeping me stocked up with pain au chocolats. It had warmed up to a near tropical minus 4 and conditions were exquisite. Every small hill took me above, and then back down into the mist. Things hurt less on days like this and the pain au chocolats were amazing. Less amazing was my French. I remember thinking that if you set up a French speaking competition between Del Boy from "Only Fools and Horses", a six year old, and myself, I'd definitely finish last. For the rest of the journey I frequently resorted to a mixture of charades and pointing to establish the likeliest path ahead. Richard and Carrie thoroughly enjoyed watching me baffle shopkeepers, policemen, and road sweepers right, left and centre as I effortlessly murdered the French language.

Powered by an enormous selection of novel bakery products I reached the van, 32.5 miles from Dieppe. I was pleased to do so, as the charge of my Garmin, which gave me an accurate readout of the exact distance travelled had almost died in the cold. We usually calculated the distance according to the satellite readings from the Garmin, and confirmed this with distances from Google pedometer, and Internet-based calculators from Map my Run or similar bits of software. The distances on the road signs seemed to correlate fairly well with these measurements in Britain, but there were often disparities in France. An example on this day was that one sign showed Montville to be 7km away, while the next one, 3km later, showed it to be 8km away. This was frustrating when trying to calculate where my next food fix could be scavenged.

What the French lack in arithmetic, they make up for in mini-marts. I raided one such establishment offering proper food and coffee as opposed to the less delightful cremated pies and sausage rolls so favoured in the UK. Wires had been pulled down from the bottom of the van by a block of ice adhering to them, and I spent a happy hour boiling water for (alternately) hot chocolate and ice block melting. I picked Susie up from the ferry, having nearly gone the wrong way round a roundabout and we had a great meal. Susie was on top form, brimming with supplies. I slept for a record ten hours that night, fatigued from the previous night's lack of shut eye.

Montville looked as I imagined a French town in winter would look. A late start, as seems traditional in France, left me scampering through the snowy streets, past boulangeries, charcuteries, and invariably into patisseries. I was eating for three and the quality of the food made this an agreeable mission. I've yet to find any research to back this up, but I'm sure French baking must be good for sore knees, as the pains had dissipated. I'd spent the previous evening reading a bit of "Born to Run", by Christopher McDougall. It's a brilliant book describing the enjoyment runners get from this ancient pursuit, as well as the Tarahumara Indians who run seemingly endless distances virtually barefoot. This fascinated me, but I'd happily keep my trainers on in the snow. What intrigued me was the mystery and freedom described by the runners. I invariably feel free and happy when I run, but this challenge had been different. I hadn't the freedom to run just when I desired as I do back home. At times I was having to run, whether I wanted to do or not! Interesting also, was the supposition that Homo Sapiens survived where the Neaderthals failed, despite Neanderthals being stronger, quicker over short distances, and having larger brains. Some think that Homo Sapiens ability to run relentlessly, and catch prey this way was the major factor dictating our survival.

Some days were fun packed, joyful affairs. This wasn't one of them as Day 27 took me through Rouen, where Joan of Arc was burnt at the stake in 1431. I found it non-descript and uninspiring, as I trudged along endless miles of docks alongside the river. A headwind had started to gust, and I'd managed to get myself lost a couple times. A combination of snow and sleet had left me soaking and cold, and the major trunk roads felt less safe. I couldn't be bothered and forced out 34.7 miles. Matters improved as we located a surprisingly cheap hotel, complete with a television. It was 3pm and it almost felt like back home watching the football, while substituting the usual beer for a Rego recovery drink. The hotel's owner was friendly but advised me not to go running tomorrow as the weather forecast was "tres terrible."

In fact the weather was only fairly terrible. I finished running early, so I could give Susie a lift back to Dieppe for her ferry. She had been a wonderful support in conditions that were treacherous to run or drive in. Ever generous, she had bought several parting gifts, including lots of food and a Christmas tree. It was December after all. The drive back fascinated me. The snow, previously piled high had virtually gone and it looked like a different world. Jennie's dad Graham arrived on the 3.30am ferry, and worst still for him, Chelsea had only drawn. We slept a few hours then set off south again. I was using every spare minute to eat, and had just about maintained my weight. I watched Mr Takeru Kobayashi of Japan on YouTube triumph in the Coney Island Hot Dog eating competition. He managed 60 hot dogs in 15 minutes, appearing to dip the bun in a vat of Sprite before forcing them down. Mr Kobayashi finally met his match when the show featured a 1089lb bear that demolished 50 bun-less hot dogs in 2 minutes 36. As a tribute I ate six large pain au chocolat, a litre of yoghurt, two bananas and some energy drink for breakfast and felt unwell. Further investigation on Wikipedia revealed Mr Kobayashi had recently eaten 8kg of cow's brain in 15 minutes, which would not be featuring on my menu. I think a Brit eating 8kg of cow brain would be way too much for the French.

The snow had started again as we were on high ground and several vehicles had become stuck. Some friendly locals had helped push the campervan out. The outside of my left knee was painful, which felt like an Iliotibial band injury. This gave me a dull pain constantly, with an occasional snap, as the tissue brushed over the bony prominence on the outside of my knee when running. I shortened my stride and tensed my abdominal muscles, which seemed to help. Almost every car that passed offered me a lift, as I ran through a National Park. 34 more miles later we were in Mamers, which merits a Wikipedia page, but has little information on it other than stating a population of 5896. This seemed remarkably precise, and I can add that it had exactly one hotel, with exactly no stars. We gorged ourselves on a menu of the day and discussed weddings briefly, before moving on to football.

The road is long, especially in winter. Photo – Richard Else

Andy and Jennie Murray

CHAPTER 12

Le Mans to the Pyrenees and the North Pole Marathon

"Polar bears rarely venture to the area, and haven't entered, so would be disqualified"

RICHARD DONOVAN

Day 30 brought rain of biblical proportions. It wasn't even worth changing clothes as I'd be soaked within five minutes. Le Mans is home to the famous Le Mans 24-Hour race, and its roads are busy. Combine this with constant standing water for a horrible experience of getting soaked from all angles. The system we used to make sure Graham and I were on the same track was to mark two maps. I would carry one and the other would be in the vehicle. I kept mine in a zip-lock bag to keep it dry, but it got soaked whenever I turned a page. This added to my trepidation for the next couple of days, which followed a similar pattern of running through the rain, warming up in the van, eating food, and repeat. On Day 31, I'd gone through the 1000-mile mark with the snow falling. My iliotibial band was chronically sore, and every couple of miles it would give me a pain that would stop me dead for a minute or so. Days like this make or break the run. Poor weather and pain are an unhappy combination, and I just willed the weather to break. I knew I couldn't complain about the prevailing wind or weather as I'd chosen to run in winter due to the timing of personal events, but surely it had to improve soon. I'm sure the injury I had was at least partly psychological, and I thought it would be interesting to study the degree that mental state correlates with perceived injury.

Graham had been fantastic and we shared some cakes before he left. He'd given up four days to get soaked in France following in the steps of a slightly grumpy future son-in-law. Having worked as an accounts manager at Tetley's for years, he made a fine cuppa, and could update me on all the important sporting matters. He'd swap with my mum at Poitiers airport. The day was crisp and clear and the wind behind me and I felt I could run forever as I jogged through quaint villages and past several hunting parties. I presume the hunters were after something less scrawny than myself and I carried on towards the Loire.

I ran into Marc who insisted I came and saw his place. He'd lived in Scotland for years and couldn't believe I'd run from there. He had his own vineyard and had a restaurant serving food almost entirely consisting of his own produce. His guest rooms included a bath large enough to splash about in. Despite only 32.5 miles on the clock this was too tempting, and I texted Mum where I'd be. Things were looking up. Marc had a fantastic part-French part-Scottish dialect, talking fondly about "wee pubs in Aviemore," but bemoaning the Scottish climate as "unsuitable for ze vineyard." He did an outstanding chicken impression, and a fantastic meat platter whilst educating us on how to grow wine, and what to feed pigs.

Life suddenly seemed almost idyllic. I crossed the partly frozen Loire with vineyards on either side, and it appeared as though there were chateaux everywhere. Swans wandered around on the frozen river looking confused in front of a Cinderalla-like castle. For the first time in a week I took a photo. Mum had washed my clothes and the land was flat. We gossiped about family matters, and she updated me on her tennis and squash teams. Life could not have been made easier for me – mum was doing practically everything for me so pushing out 34 miles was straightforward. My good friend Joe Symonds was to join me for a week's running. I relished the prospect of company, and with Joe's background in elite running, I doubted the distances would be a problem to him. The loneliness of the long distance runner is over-rated. We caught up and chatted about everything and nothing. Joe did the navigation, and the mental pressure was relieved. I'm not an elite runner, and when I shared a flat with Joe, I wasn't even the quickest in my flat. We hadn't caught up properly for ages, and he'd recently become engaged.

(Top left) The helmet cam attracting plenty of strange looks. (Top right) The faithful campervan. (Bottom left and right) Hitting the road

He grinned like a cat whenever talking about Esther, and embarrassingly for two blokes we talked about weddings almost more than about football. Joe and his brother Andy had added the Original Mountain Marathon to all sorts of other wins while I'd been in Indonesia, and we laughed and compared notes about previous races. Apparently they had squeezed past Jethro Lennox and his partner with minutes to go. Nothing beats grabbing an improbable victory. I personally love the games that Aberdeen win 2-1 with a last minute penalty more than the all too rare 3-nils. I'd read his dad Hugh's excellent book *Running High*, which featured a very young Joe and Andy following their dad around in a campervan.

In this part of France it would be rude not to enjoy the odd glass of wine, and we picked up some wine from a local vineyard. Although the distance was still arduous I'd look forward to getting the legs moving each morning. Mum was extremely attentive and had miraculously succeeded in getting me to gain weight this week, despite me running over 34 miles every day. There were two occasions I overdid it, and ended up filling the bin with my previous meal. We also spent time in semi-rural hotels, often with a pleasant restaurant serving wine. Mum seemed to relish a spell between the Loire and Dordogne, and tucked into a different French style meal every night. She gave everything a go, although her face dropped when the tripe salad was served at a railway station.

The iliotibial band injury was improving. Joe was carrying the same injury, although complained a lot less often. Iliotibial band syndrome is a common injury in long distance runners, and is difficult to settle down without resting it. I'd previously had Iliotibial band syndrome after competing in a race while wearing snow shoes at the North Pole. The snow shoes are so wide that the mechanics of running is completely altered which had been at the root of the problem in the Arctic. Various stretching exercises helped then, and while this option was not available running on the Arctic Ocean, using smaller, flatter roads in France was helping. We ran on tiny roads, virtually vehicle free, and I'm sure there would be a market to sell running tours from the Loire towards Bordeaux. Participants could stay in fantastic chateaus, drink fine wine, and jog through some of France's most astounding countryside. This felt like the easiest week of the trip, with great company, great scenery and great weather.

I felt a momentum swing behind me. The hospitality continued to astound us, other than at one meal where we were served by a lady with a remarkable resemblance to Cruella De Vil. Everything was too much trouble for her, including ordering a glass of water, and putting the heater on. The final straw was when Mum ordered a medium cooked steak, which apparently equated to high treason. She muttered something about, "you Brits, always ruining food" or something similar then snarled off. We could not confirm any sinister interest in Dalmations and in fairness the food was great but she was undoubtedly the least accommodating host this side of Fawlty Towers.

Images from the Loire Valley

(Top left) Helmet cam. (Bottom left and right) Running, and the obligatory wine tasting with Joe Symonds. Photos – Mary Murray

Half Way   Scotland 2 Sahara Blog

I'm in sight of the Pyrenees. Amazingly beautiful, and also a bit scary looking at the snow at 500 metres. I've now done 1348.6 miles (to be precise) in 41 days, and am a couple days away only before setting foot in Spain. John O Groats seems a long way away, and it is. This week mum has been out keeping me fed and the van tidier than when im in charge. Prior to that i had future father in law Graham Reeves, brilliant to catch up with Graham and i havent scuppered my hopes of marrying jennie yet. I've succeeded in putting a little weight on this week, which is quite impressive given ive run 34 miles as a minimum, with over 240 miles for the week. The week has taken me from North of the Loire, through major wine country, down through Bordeaux and the dordogne, and the Parc National de Gascogne. Heading towards Biarritz tomorrow. I've had Joe Symonds for running company this week, and have almost certainly bored him senseless with a 5 weeks of banal conversation i have been especially storing up. However i have won a bet to subject him to more pickled eggs, and know the latin for goose bumps and all the breeds of penguins.

The Dordogne is one of the most popular regions of France for a reason. It was stunning, and the wine was superb. We even received curious expressions from the vineyard cat as we sampled reds in our shorts with the temperatures below freezing. I'm very much from the 'fill her up' school of wine tasting, and can hardly tell a Cab Sav from a Buckfast, but even I could tell this stuff was good. Having three people in the van made the accommodation quite tight, but it didn't rain at all so didn't matter. The day Joe left I worked out I'd run over 50 marathons in 40 days. I was almost half way. This should have been the easy half. It was all mountains and hills from now on!

With the physio help Joe had given and running on dry roads, which allowed me to run on the flat part of the road, the injury situation had improved. As expected, with only the night to recover, injuries never completely healed but they were miles better, and I could run freely. I'd lost less than half a kilo overall, testament to my support crew and the fine French food. Things were looking good – my future wife was coming out to join me, nothing could be better.

I ran 34 miles and felt great, and could have run much further but I knew there was still a long way to the Sahara. The mighty snow-clad Pyrenees reared into view like a colossal white barrier. As if guarding the mountains, a sizeable dog bounded up snarling furiously. Wearing the head-cam I tried not to act too scared. The Pyrenees were immense, forming an unbroken line as far as the eye could see but perhaps things were going too well.

My phone rang. It was Jennie. "My flight's cancelled. There's masses of snow and it's getting worse. I don't know when I'll get to France."

In pleasant conditions in the south of France it seemed surreal that Britain was at a standstill due to snow. My thoughts went back to when I ran past a closed Gatwick Airport. What could we do? How could we get Jennie out here? Would Mum's flights be cancelled too?

To clear my head I ran another three miles. This was terrible news. No flights were going at all apparently, and the snow was set to continue. I felt so far away, so distant. The forecast suggested there would be no flights the next day and that a train, from London to Spain, would be the quickest option. This sounded like no fun whatsoever. Mum's flight was also cancelled, but we hoped to find a flight to Edinburgh, which appeared to be more snow-free than Southern England. Much telephoning and surfing the web ensued, and ultimately we found a flight for Mum. This was a tremendous relief as Mum, like myself, is a GP and cancelling whole clinics is difficult, and all GP's absolutely hate doing it. Mum was giving her all to the project, dedicated and unassuming, and usually smiling, and I felt I was letting her down by not getting her back to work in time. It's impossible to quantify the sacrifices parents make to help their children, but Mum invariably goes far beyond the call of duty. I was glad she'd get home, having obviously taken pleasure and satisfaction from her week in France.

The whole situation with the tight and ever changing transport arrangements took me back to a manic week in 2007. Mum and I had spent many hours battling to find a way to get me from the Sahara Desert to an interview, and then up to the North Pole, and all within three days.

During the GP selection interview, I had been asked where I was working at present.

"I'm working all over the place, doing a whole mix of things," I replied.

"Ok, and where are you working this week?" the interviewer asked.

"I've a flight in an hour. I'm working at the North Pole."

On the flight to Longyearbyen, where competitors would assemble prior to the flight transfer to the North Pole, I reflected on a busy week in my life.

Twelve days previously I'd been in Argentina, having come down from the summit of Mt Aconcagua, at 6962 metres or 22241 feet, the highest mountain in South America and the highest mountain outside of Asia. Jennie and I had topped out together to reveal South America and clouds beneath us. I'd come down with a full camera, but five kilogrammes of muscle mass lighter.

The next destination on this extreme backpacking tour, as my friend Paul Liebenberg labelled it, was the Marathon des Sables (MDS). Completing it is seen as a badge of honour in the ultra running community, and it was to be my first ultra marathon. This race is divided into 6 stages. In addition to that, competitors have to carry everything they will need for the duration (apart from a tent) on their backs in a rucksack. This includes all food, cooking equipment and clothing. Water is rationed and handed out at checkpoints, and there is no prospect of popping to the shops if you forget something.

I was a shambles. Mt Aconcagua was not the best place to garner supplies for this 151-mile multiday desert race, and I was hopelessly underprepared, turning up in an Argentina football shirt, surf shorts, and a huge rucksack. I had bought loads of carbohydrate powder when briefly in the UK, but bought much of my other food from the market in Morocco. This race is dominated by the Moroccans in general, and particularly the legendary Ahansal brothers, who have won 14 of the last 15 races between them. Hailing from the desert, they glide through the stifling heat and sand and looked very different from me at the start line with tiny backpacks and desert clothes.

It took lashings of good luck, and sound advice to get me through this masochistic exercise. I was fortunate to be taken aside and given some hints and supplies by some kindly competitors who had experienced this race before, and considered my kit with a sympathetic smile. The history of the race reveals that others have been less fortunate. In 1994, Italian policeman Mauro Prosperi apparently lost his way in a sandstorm, and was discovered barely alive and 13kg lighter several days later. Unfortunately the year I was there, a competitor passed away in his sleep, despite being a fine runner and being well prepared.

I finished about 50th out of 900 and left disappointed with myself. Most had prepared thoroughly, and achieved what they were capable of. It's said that perfect preparation prevents poor performance, and I hadn't given the event the respect it deserved. I vowed to return to the desert and put things right.

A couple of the competitors in my tent perfectly illustrated what the MDS is all about: preparation, guts and mental strength. Alan Silcock had failed to finish the year prior. This year he'd trained to exhaustion and had the perfect, and very lightweight kit. Each day our tent mates applauded him back to the tent as he crossed the finish line, chalking off another destructive day. Despite crater-sized blisters, he spent most of his time chatting contentedly.

Marathon des Sables tent mates. Standing, from left: Cliff, Malcolm, me, Alan, Joe, Lynsey. Seated from left: Shaun and Paul
Photo – Alan Silcock

Malcolm is a New Zealander and came to the event hoping to finish well up the field. He'd complained of shin splints when I'd run with him on the first two days. With 70 miles of racing still to go he clutched his leg in agony. It was apparent to me he had stress fractured his tibia, the major bone in his lower leg. That would be curtains for him. Amazingly he dragged himself to the finish that day, and every other day. Although his determination damaged his leg so severely that he was required to wear a plaster cast for six months, his resolve and commitment were extraordinary. Everyone saw him grimace and his leg bend when he performed the Maori Haka at the end. My subsequent experience of running a far shorter distance through the Arctic with this fracture still leaves me shaking my head.

The shower blocks in Ouarzazate took a hammering, as 900 desert racers besieged them following a week without a wash, before everyone limped round the dance floors of local hostelries.

The Highway to Hell. Photo – Alan Silcock

My flight to Britain was cancelled. I spent a frantic hour at Marrakesh airport explaining that I had my interview in 12 hours time, and a delay of more than five hours would cause me to miss it. I cursed myself for cutting everything so fine, and was honestly more relieved than I was at the MDS finish when a flight was found for me.

I'd be working at the North Pole, as well as running. Participants tested their equipment, as well as going dog-sled racing at 78 degrees north, where the cold was sufficient to cause frost nip in minutes. Flying from Norway to the Pole, I knew I was in for the experience of a lifetime. It is a remarkable race in every way, run not on land, but the frozen water of the Arctic Ocean. I found it baffling that we would be running on water, at 90 degrees north latitude, literally at the top of the world. The race organiser Richard Donovan is an understated but impressive man.

His eloquence in relating his achievements of being the first man to run marathons at the North and South Poles and the horrific conditions he encountered were discussed with breathtaking simplicity. Richard pioneered the route, running it solo in 2002. Since then he has run a marathon on all seven continents within five days and ten hours, won races in the Himalaya, over the Inca Trail, and many more worldwide, often in extreme climactic conditions. He is completely unassuming with this, but took great delight in describing to competitors the potential hazards at the Pole. Extreme sub zero conditions would await, and the course would be checked for holes in the ice. Snowshoes were advisable, as the snow would be "difficult to run through." Polar bears rarely venture to the area, but had not officially entered the race so would be disqualified. Staff had weapons to fire in the air, should any bear appear. The course, being floating ice, was constantly moving, and a runway for the Antanov jet had been prepared. The contrast with the Sahara Desert was absolute.

The Geographic North Pole is 430miles from the nearest land, the uninhabited Kaffeklubben island off the north coast of Greenland. The sea depth has been estimated at 4261metres, and the ice is between six and 12 feet thick on average. The sun only sets, and rises, once a year. Although these facts were interesting, all I could think about was keeping warm!

The race started and I immediately tripped over my snowshoes. I'd layered up in conditions of minus 25 Celcius, and the width of the showshoes, and the balaclava, made progress difficult. Hillocks of hard packed ice were split by softer snow, which felt like running through treacle. The ice slapped off the Arctic Ocean with every step. It was surreal, and having used a weather window to arrive at the Pole we were running in broad daylight at 2.45am. The food and water I had carried were frozen solid. The course consisted of ten laps of a marked course, with a tent serving warm water. I felt like I was on a different planet.

The race was won by elite ultra runner Tommy Maguire in record time. I was fourth and was pleased that neither I nor the Russian doctor had seen much in the way of frostbite on the runners. The first mountain bike race to take place at the Pole, the North Pole Bike Extreme took place almost immediately afterwards.

This race utilised the cut runway, but cycling conditions were exacting. Spiked tyres gripped and rolled, propelling riders onward but riding was phenomenally arduous. Risks of frostbite in the hands and feet were much higher during the bike race, as these limbs moved less than during the marathon, although no lasting injuries were sustained. I doubt a hardier group of adventurers assembles for a marathon anywhere else on earth, and it was an honour being part of the event.

Perhaps the most amazing achievement was that of Paralympic athlete William Tan. He used the specially-prepared flat runway section of the course to complete a marathon in a wheelchair, covering his particular circuit in just over 21 hours. William is also a doctor and we got on well. He'd contracted polio when he was two, and had discovered his athletic talent as a teenager. His 'can do' attitude was reflected in the vast sums of money he has raised for charity, and the time he invests in helping others. In typical understated fashion he told me "it was way harder than a normal marathon. Even on the runway it's impossible to free wheel." The image of William completing his marathon at the North Pole showed me two things that were life changing. The human body and mind can work with conditions that at first glance would seem completely unsuitable (I must admit I initially doubted anyone could complete a wheelchair marathon at the Pole,) and that there is no point in feeling sorry, or making excuses for yourself. Almost anything is possible with preparation, resolve and perseverance. I'd need to plan more carefully, and work harder if I wanted to do better.

Back on the *Scotland2Sahara* challenge, my planning had fallen by the wayside but the Triple Echo/ BBC team again could not have been more helpful. Team member Paul Diffley was on the way to a Mountain Film Festival in Spain to pick up the event's top award. He would most helpfully drive the van over the foothills and into Spain so I didn't have to carry my gear over the hills. That meant I didn't have to backtrack to get the van. This made all the difference, and knowing Jennie was safely on the train to Spain, I crossed the border with a huge smile on my face. Goodbye to my old friend pain au chocolat and hello to chorizo and the mountains.

Prior to setting out, I hadn't appreciated fully the beauty and topography of Spain. I had realised the Pyrenees would be a treat for the eyes, if not the legs. The long

Running the North Pole Marathon. Photo – Mike King/ North Pole Marathon

climbs up into the Pyrenees left me wondering how the Tour de France cyclists manage these climbs day in and day out. I was about to find out. I was also relieved there was virtually no snow on the road. A big concern had been getting blocked by the snow, and having got over the initial pass and seeing valleys and mountains in all directions I felt like I'd stepped out of a wardrobe and was in the snowy and hilly forest of Narnia.

The only ever bike race at the North Pole. Photo – Mike King/North Pole Marathon

CHAPTER 13

The Pyrenees to Guadalajara Including Christmas

"It wasn't a normal Christmas."

Paul and I drove down from the mountains to find Jennie. We'd booked into a hotel to allow us some decent sleep. I was so glad to see Jennie since we had so much to catch up on, and the next morning we drove back up into the Pyrenees. There were several up and downs on the route that day equating to over 1000 metres of ascent. Birds of prey circled above me as I took a minor road high into the snow to avoid the tunnels. These tunnels had quickly become a nemesis of mine. Pedestrians were banned from them because of safety issues, and to get over them I had to scramble over the hillside, which was often covered in thorns or dense scrub. I usually emerged resembling the loser in a cat fight. Once over the top it was a long downhill into Pamplona, home of the 'running of the bulls'. The downhill was exhilarating and the excitement of a new country was still tangible. The last time we'd been in Spain was when Jennie had been running in Andalusia. I'd been one of the race doctors, and Spain had won the football World Cup while we were there. I had my Spain strip on, but this time the boot was on the other foot – I was running and Jennie was looking after me!

My Spanish is probably worse than my French, and asking for directions could be a long drawn out affair. There are fewer small towns than in France or England, so by necessity more time would need to be spent on bigger roads.

Offsetting this, by heading south the daylight would get longer as we had now passed December 21st, the shortest day of the year. This seemed like a turning point however imperceptible the change would be, meaning I could lie in longer in the mornings if I felt like it.

I'd always associated Spain with San Miguel, beaches and paella, and I can now add beautiful mountains to this vision of the country. When the weather was clear, mountains filled the horizons. There were amazing places to free camp too and I particularly remember Per Alta, where we camped high over the village, and the majestic Cervera Del Rio Alhama. Cervera huddles in a narrow high sided gorge where caves pock-mark the sides of the canyon. Apparently the locals used to live in them. A myriad of birds of prey circled in the thermals above a wonderful sunset and I could feel my body and resolve strengthening. For the first time we discussed the possibility of increasing my daily distance where able, to avoid having large unsupported stretches in Morocco at the end. Being truly solo would be OK, although it would be significantly harder in the desert where I would have to carry 9 litres of water a day, as well as all my other gear, and sand is difficult enough to run through without dragging a sledge. I felt capable of increasing my daily distances, and I had managed to maintain my weight, but doing this over the mountainous terrain that remained would be hard. Without fail I could now run the first 26-30 miles comfortably, and then would begin to tire.

As a kind of encouragement, the climb out of Cervera stayed with me for a long time. A tiny road clung to the side of the gorge, hair-pinning its way vertiginously skyward and the river that created this ravine was hardly visible 500 metres below. We had a picnic at the top, and I found the trip's first strong tailwind. It was an incredible feeling, almost flying into the valley, before settling down to another lengthy climb up to a 1150 metre viewpoint for the second time that day. I'd almost forgotten it was Christmas Eve.

35.5 miles later we parked up next to a stable. This seemed marvellously biblical as we shared some wine and put the presents under the van's little Christmas tree. Being high in the Sierra it was formidably cold and it began to snow as we anticipated an unusual Christmas. I reflected on my friends and family.

Christmas Day in the campervan. 38 miles done and ready for dinner. Photo – Jennie Murray

Despite the lack of physical proximity, I felt so close to them through their frequent encouragements, and knowing that their thoughts and prayers were with us. It felt an appropriate day to consider all that God had given us.

Santa had been kind to me. My main gift was having Jennie with me, and I got a good tailwind into the bargain. There were other presents too, and the van bulged with discarded wrapping paper as I left Jennie to play with her new toys. I pretended to be upset that she'd forgotten her Christmas CD's, but I greedily munched chocolate Santas at most stops, and gobbled every festive snack I could. The tailwind propelled me 38.3 miles over rolling countryside that was festively complete with shepherds, to finish at a church. We'd managed to catch up with families during the day and although we both missed having the rest of our loved ones around us, I appreciated what I had. A roast turkey would be impossible to cook on the two gas hobs we had in the van, but traditional Spanish sausages and mash couldn't be bettered. We stopped in a layby and watched shooting stars with a glass of wine in hand. It was a great end to what had been a marvellous Christmas.

Boxing Day broke with a Siberian chill. The gauge read minus nine and the diesel engine started very slugglishly. Two young girls had a good laugh at me as I took to the road and at around 10am the conditions warmed up considerably. Cruising along by foot allowed me to take more in than had I been driving – I could almost feel the heartbeat of the land! Seeing a herd of deer in the hills reminded me of home and I suddenly recalled a similar scene the day Jennie and I were engaged. On several occasions I was offered oranges by complete strangers, acts of kindness which displayed a generosity of spirit that seemed to be prevalent in Spain. I ran 35 miles on Boxing Day, then 33.5 the next day, which was perfect distance-wise for the town of Guadalajara. Despite having access to plenty of boiling water, six days on the road had left me smelling positively ripe so checking into a hotel with a bath was an unimaginable luxury and certainly reduced the assault on Jennie's nose.

Once in the hotel I was astounded to see the number of messages that had been left for me on Facebook and Twitter. I suspect many folk thought of me pounding out the miles as they enjoyed their Christmas dinner, and several very generous donations seemed to reflect this. By now I'd covered 1658.9 miles, leaving only

1000 miles, or just over 38 marathons, still to run. Bizarrely, I felt I was entering the home stretch. Thanks to the luxurious bath I could no longer smell myself, but I had certainly caught a whiff of the finish.

Christmas Day view in Spain

CHAPTER 14

Guadalajara to Brazatortas

"I was sure I was becoming anaemic."

Guadalajara is approximately 65 kilometres north-east of Madrid and as I crossed the Hernares River I imagined running into Madrid the next day. Mark Beaumont, in his captivating book "The Man Who Cycled the World", describes how he got a police escort through Madrid, and suggests it is a very busy city. Latest statistics put the population of the greater metropolitan area at 5.8 million, the third largest in Europe. My previous visit to Madrid had been in the guise of supporting Aberdeen Football Club three years before when they had played Athletico Madrid and I had found it to be an incredible city with rich traditions, fine architecture and a number of excellent hostelries. The locals had been suitably bemused by several thousand fans dressed in red or as sheep, or in my case Sherlock Holmes, for no reason in particular. I'd been roundly baffled by street signs and how to get home. Thus I played it safe and skirted the city on this occasion, feeling sure I would return next time Aberdeen played Real Madrid.

We stocked up the van with anything our hearts desired and watched football on TV in the evening. Madrid is reputably fairly dry, and it hadn't rained for almost a week. Conditions were almost ideal with temperatures of 5-10 degrees during the day, and no clothes to dry off. I wondered whether the worst of the weather was now behind us?

Campervan life

My research showed some interesting results so far, indicating that there had been only three days when I hadn't complained of any injury, and that the severity of these injuries was beginning to improve. It was an encouraging trend, and I also noticed that I had kept my weight pretty stable and didn't need to sleep so much. Almost perpetual fatigue had accompanied the first two weeks of the run, with the running having to compete with the demands of studying and planning events.

Typical Spanish hill country

I would battle on through the mornings, and then have some 'wake up juice' with lunch. The original recipe for this delicacy according to Back to the Future's Emmett Brown, includes green olive juice, Tabasco sauce, cayenne pepper, chilli pepper, onion and mustard seeds. My more prosaic version consisted of a couple of paracetamols, a can of Red Bull and a can of Coke. This had seemed to enliven me enough to run for another hour when required to in Scotland, but I'd used it more sparingly since. I had experimented with Brown's recipe during my university days, but with rather lively consequences for my stomach.

Noblejas stands out as a place I wouldn't want to live. I have to admit the fact that it took such an effort to get there didn't help its cause in any way. The route on our map appeared to roll down a long hill past a spectacular turret of rocks to a river, before climbing up to a town whose description had sounded elegant and contemporary. As it transpired, the bridge to the minor road was down, and a monotonous slog up a motorway sized road ensued. I was stopped by the police who could not comprehend why anybody would want to run on such a road, (and probably why anyone would voluntarily be heading towards Noblejas) and who simply shrugged their shoulders when I tried to explain. Entering the ugliest industrial estate I've ever seen, two more policemen asked similar questions and offered me a few oranges, presumably by way of compensation. We camped away from the smoke belching factories, and had a beer. The festive season remained in full swing, and I enjoyed a steak of humongous proportions while we watched the Spanish enjoy their celebrations.

Making swift my escape from Noblejas the following morning, I realised there were only two days left of 2010. I'd had the chance to check my emails, and it appeared the UK was gearing up for a great New Year party. Looking at the map, we'd be miles from anywhere, and even playing with the route wouldn't find us a town. As I stretched off my hamstring, which I'd pulled slightly, I thought about what the next year would bring. In the past two months every experience and emotion had appeared to be grossly magnified. Lows were difficult to shake off, and the highs were amazing, and each day usually consisted of a combination of both. My hamstring was tight, but anti-inflammatory gel and ice was helping, along with the stretching. I felt nauseas with the volume of food I'd just eaten, but experience had taught me that spectacular views and good times wouldn't be far away. I stopped running on December 30th immediately prior to a thunderstorm and later, from the warmth of a local bar, we heard the rain lashing against the corrugated iron roof.

Around the hills of Mora, literally millions of olive trees stretch out in every direction. Watching the farmers beating the trees to harvest the olives, between endless cigarettes had fascinated me. I hadn't realised how labour intensive the process was, and presumed it would be mechanised. I'd grabbed a couple of olives from a tree thinking they'd be perfect and fresh to eat, but as the farmer explained they were being harvested before they were fully ripe. We camped overlooking the valley and woke to the sound of rain slapping off the van roof.

Hogmanay, or New Year's Eve, is not one I usually spend running ultra marathons. The bonus was that it was "probably mostly downhill except for the uphill bit," as Jennie explained. The finale to the year's running involved a sweeping downhill onto a lake shore, with kingfishers, storks, and herons patrolling slate grey water surrounded by fir trees. The incessant drizzle was reminiscent of home and we had Scottish oatcakes, with English jam, French wine, and Spanish chorizo and olives. The wind continually raked across the lake, and birds squawked their dismay at the stormy conditions as we dined in the van. In the quietest New Year in my memory, we were in bed by ten o'clock. We didn't even manage to wake at midnight to toast in the New Year with a glass of wine.

Next morning felt like Groundhog Day rather than the New Year. Breakfast, run, eat, run, eat, run, plan, sleep. This was the basis for the day, as it had been for the previous 53 days. I ran through 15 miles of drizzle prior to finding the first town, and the locals looked decidedly sorry for themselves. In essentially a friendly and vibrant country, there were no smiles in this town, as people shuffled about in the rain looking positively morose. I bent into the wind praying for a return to sunshine.

Ciudad Real was a tempting 18 miles from where we had finished on New Year's Day. Boasting hotels with showers and restaurants we passed the Don Quiote Arena on the way in. The real reason we stayed in Ciudad Real was so I could use the Internet, as I suspected I was starting to become anaemic. The symptoms were interesting. I had become more breathless running at the same speed, and much more tired despite running the standard 34-35 daily miles. It was frustrating because I was suffering fewer injuries, and thought I could crank up the mileage a bit.

Finding a computer I checked out the local clinics online, and pondered my options. After further thought, I guessed that while I was almost certainly slightly anaemic, and while I had been taking vitamins to keep my iron stores up, my current iron intake wasn't adequate enough. A common side effect of iron tablets is nausea and vomiting, and I often felt sick after taking these tablets, so I decided the best time to take them would be at night, once I'd eaten all my food for the day. I would avoid blood tests for the moment, and only have them if things deteriorated further. Jennie had actually mentioned how pale I looked, and it had irritated me that this was obvious to others also. If this deterioration continued, the mountains of Morocco could literally prove insurmountable, as less oxygen is available in the air at altitude, making having a normal blood count even more critical. That night we went for a relatively romantic meal, ate plenty tapas, and I had two iron tablets for dessert. The Spanish eat relatively late, so we had no problem finding a great restaurant at 10.30pm.

The splendidly named Brazatortas was the target for Day 56. All day we travelled through a seemingly endless traverse of olive groves, which eventually broke up over the hilltops, giving a magnificent view into what I presumed was Andalusia. The jagged outline of the mountains in the distance contrasted with the rolling character of the landscapes we had just travelled through but despite the scenery, having convinced myself of being anaemic, I found this day mentally difficult. I was even reduced to walking up one of the steeper inclines. A few niggles had flared up, which I think were as much due to my mental weakness that day rather than any serious physical impediment, and I vomited twice in the afternoon, possibly as a consequence of taking an iron tablet at lunch.

CHAPTER 15

Brazatortas to Algeciras and the Everest Marathon

"Everest. It's only a mountain."

JUNKO TABEI

Day 57 would finish in Andalusia, one of the most verdant and beautiful provinces in Spain. I had friends in this area and today I'd meet Volker and Encarna who had recently got married. I work at events with Volker, and he'd hoped to run a day with me, but his crutches told us this wouldn't be possible. They had appeared through the mist with Scotland hats and Spanish flags on. They had brought some traditional Spanish food, and it was a pleasing change to have company for both Jennie and I. Jennie was uncomplaining, but I could sense she had a bit of cabin fever spending practically 24 hours a day in the van, and doing the vast majority of the cooking. It was a memorable day also for the afternoon's clear blue skies, high mountain passes, wild pigs, and picnics. It was the first day we could properly laze about in the sun, and Jennie came running, which I think offered her an insight into Spain's hills.

The 36 miles landed us in Torrecampo, in the province of Andalusia. An Andalusian speciality is pork, and it was not difficult to imagine why, with pigs happily roaming the lush hillside pastures. That evening we dined on pork and more pork, along with other fresh Andalusian specialities served in a rustic farmhouse whilst reminiscing about old times.

Father and son in Ronda. Photo – Mary Murray

The company cheered us immeasurably, and I resolved to increase my daily mileage to 36 per day. Although the land was downright mountainous, its captivating beauty made running simple. The essence of the challenge was to push myself hard and take in the views, and I felt that southern Spain and Morocco were a perfect environment to continue this, and attempt to push the envelope further. The worries of my potential anaemia seemed trivial in the sunlight.

A partial solar eclipse added further excitement. Jennie and I watched from a petrol station with Juan the proprietor who enthusiastically explained the eclipse in Spanish of which I understood only a few words. My mind drifted to Tintin, and his heroic rescue of Captain Haddock and Professor Calculus by predicting an eclipse to their Incan captors. I'd hope to avoid a fate similar to Tintin in Morocco when the temperamental Captain Haddock attempted to pull his head off thinking he was a bottle of champagne when suffering delusions due to a combination of rum and the sun. So excited was Juan, I half expected him to morph into Haddock and complain of "blistering barnacles" or "thundering typhoons" or similar. Following this astronomical phenomenon, Juan enquired what we were doing in Spain, and was thrilled by the *Scotland2Sahara* concept. Such was his delight that he attempted to empty his shop into our van for "supplies." An inordinate amount of gifts were refused politely, but unusual items accepted included a pumpkin, elastic bands, coffee and some Spanish confectionery. I departed from this prodigious and most bizarre display of generosity with Juan and a couple motorists waving manically and beeping their car horns.

Juan had also furnished us with a route he recommended, which took me over a viewing point looking towards the imposing Sierra Nevada mountains which piled skyward to heights of 3700 metres. I wouldn't cross the Sierra Nevada, but took some time just staring at them across the smaller hills I would negotiate. I feel at home in mountain terrain, and in many ways my genesis as a runner began at the Everest Marathon. Mountains were what I was used to, and only the Straits of Gibraltar, and several ranges of mountains separated me from the Sahara. I felt I'd come full circle.

Dad and Chris showing me how it's done.

I'd taken part in the 2005 Everest Marathon. The event is listed by the Guinness Book of World Records as the highest marathon in the world. It was the first major run I took part in I and could not have chosen a more spectacular one to start with.

I'd become fascinated with the race while backpacking in Nepal. A friend and I had trekked into the Annapurna Sanctuary, a cathedral of mountain scenery, with nine peaks soaring over 7000 metres in a mind blowing 360 degree panorama. The views had amazed me, but cloud lingered over the highest peaks. Having climbed six miles down from the sanctuary, it became apparent my friend had left some valuables behind. I offered to go back and fetch these items, knowing that the clouds had cleared and the views back in the sanctuary would astound me. I jogged the six miles and 1000 metres ascent back up to the Santuary where the views were incredible. There wasn't a cloud in the sky, and the mesmerising shapes of the Annapurna range, and Machhupuchhare (or Fish Tail Mountain as it is better known due to its shape) loomed imposingly. Avalanches crashed down their white flanks. I had agreed to meet Billie at the trailhead, and jogged the 14 miles downhill, enjoying every minute. I got chatting to a porter who was the only other man running. He mentioned the Everest Marathon, declaring the scenery to be a match for Annapurna, and that was it. I decided there and then I had to take part.

Namche Bazaar – the Sherpa capital. Photo – Mark Hawker/Everest Marathon

Mt preparation was far from ideal. I'd never run a marathon before, and felt running a 'normal' one might be advisable prior to taking on one at high altitude. I was living in Australia at the time, so I chose the Melbourne Marathon. Many of my friends would agree that I enjoy playing pranks – the sad thing is I am not very good at them. I had done four weeks training for the Melbourne Marathon and I felt good. A friend of mine, who had recently attacked me with several eggs was walking down the street. I wanted to take revenge so I climbed up a ten-foot wall, and waited. As he passed, I pounced. Unfortunately for my big toe, and my first metatarsal (another bone in my foot) he saw me coming and ducked. I landed badly with an X-ray revealing breaks in two bones in my foot. This was only six weeks before the Melbourne event, and almost immediately after that I was due to go to Nepal.

Furious with myself, I didn't even consider cancelling, and although I couldn't train at all for five weeks due to the fractures I was engrossed by the history of the Everest region, and the race itself. I discovered that the marathon was founded in 1985 when an impromptu race involving ten participants took place. They had all been trekking in the Everest region. The route has subsequently been measured, and changed, and participants now race from Gorak Shep (the old Everest Base Camp at 5184m) to the Sherpa capital of Namche Bazaar (3446m) in the Khumbu region of Nepal. There has been considerable Scottish success at the race, with Jack Maitland winning in 1989, and Angela Mudge winning the ladies event in 2007, but the Nepalese now completely dominate the men's race, due to their natural ability and their superior acclimatisation. Legendary Nepali runner Hari Roka won the race for three consecutive races and is the current course record holder, running 3.50.23 in 1999.

All non-Nepali runners met in Kathmandu and trekked to the start line together, while taking in the incredible views of the region. This 'walk-in' enabled the race doctors to monitor fitness and acclimatisation throughout the trek. Contrary to popular opinion, athletes don't acclimatise better or faster than anyone else, but tend to be more ambitious with their schedules, so can often encounter altitude related problems. There was a palpable sense of excitement as all the competitors assembled for the race briefings. It was a particularly battle hardened and fit looking crowd, with almost everyone sharing tales of racing in seemingly impossible environments. I loved meeting these guys, and hearing stories that sounded like part of a film.

A flight had taken us from Kathmandu to Lukla, the gateway to the Everest region. Having rather enjoyed the flight, glimpsing Mt Everest itself amongst this abode of snow, others looked distinctly green. It emerged that immediately prior to take off, the airport mechanic had stopped the twin propeller plane, and spent a vigorous two minutes hammering the propeller back into a safer position before giving the thumbs up signal. I was glad to have missed this, but did see a plane wreck that had veered off the steep hilltop runway some years before.

The pre-marathon trek was exhilarating. Highlights included ascending Gokyo Ri, and Kala Pattar (5623m), two viewpoints that offered heavenly vistas across the highest mountain range on earth. Sherpas, who hauled supplies uncomplainingly for us, leaving us with only light rucksacks, did much of the hard work. For one day of the trek, I swapped loads with one of these lads, and only lasted half a day. They are without doubt some of the hardiest, and most disarming of people. Many of our Sherpas had climbed Everest itself, and discussed it as if it were merely a hard shift in a beautiful office. Runners are encouraged (but not obliged) to raise money for the Everest Marathon Fund, which supports health and educational projects in rural Nepal. To date, over £520,000 has been raised and I was gladdened to use this run to fund raise for such a worthy cause.

Huddling on the start line I felt nervous. I'd hobbled around the Melbourne Marathon, and my foot felt fine, but was four weeks of training realistically enough to allow me to complete one of, if not the most gruelling, marathons on earth? I'd helped a little with the medical team and was glad almost every competitor had made the start line, a challenge in itself. At altitude there is less oxygen in the air that we breathe, so we attempt to compensate for this in a variety of ways. Having less oxygen makes any form of exercise, never mind running a marathon, very difficult indeed.

Himalayan scenery

During the course of the trek, several of the competitors had developed Acute Mountain Sickness, with symptoms often including headache, nausea, and fatigue. Many said it felt like the equivalent of a bad hangover and had been treated by the doctors. Three people had been sufficiently unwell that they could not make it to Everest Base Camp. While unpleasant in itself, Acute Mountain Sickness is a sign that you are at risk of the more serious High Altitude Pulmonary Edema (HAPE), or High Altitude Cerebral Edema (HACE.) Both are life-threatening conditions which can be fatal within hours. A friend called Justin had developed HAPE, which is an excess of fluid on the lungs. He had become breathless, with pink spit, and suffered extreme fatigue. Fortunately no one in the group suffered from HACE, which is fluid on the brain, and manifests as severe headache, confusion, vomiting, and other symptoms. For both of these conditions, the treatment includes immediate descent to a lower altitude, bottled oxygen or a pressure bag if available, and medications that may include Acetazolamide, Dexamethasone, and Nifedipine. Justin had fortunately recovered sufficiently to re-ascend and start the race.

It was early morning and parky at minus 15 Celcius. There was a little snow and ice around the paths. I was wearing all my compulsory kit, including three layers of clothing, while immediately prior to the start the Nepalese runners stripped to shorts and Tee-shirts. The gun went and the Nepalese streamed into the distance. I felt my lungs were going to burst even when some rare flat ground was found. I couldn't believe how rapidly the Nepalese ran, floating over the rough terrain and blasting down debris ridden slopes instead of the switchback path. I was enchanted by this almost superhuman ability as much as their beaming smiles at the finish. When the sun rose, the air warmed rapidly so I stripped down to shorts and climbed a switchback. Although the course is predominantly downhill, there are some beastly climbs to contend with. On the first major climb I tried to run, but due to a lack of acclimatisation to the low oxygen levels, I began to get tunnel vision and was forced to power walk. I mentally ticked off checkpoints, which were at three-mile intervals and continued past monasteries, villages, and a world of mountains on the rough path to Namche Bazaar.

Things had been going well enough, but I knew that with my lack of training I was bound to 'blow up' at some point. Despite this, I pushed on. What could beat the feeling of such a physical challenge in one of the world's most stunning environments? Despite a couple of falls and impending exhaustion I was progressing through the field. I heard reports that a Sherpa had finished, when I still had six miles to go, which proved to be an undulating loop finishing in Namche Bazaar. The Sherpa capital is hardly New York, but it looked like a metropolis following two weeks in the high hills. I caught Adrian Davis, a fellow

Mt Everest (left)

Scot, with 500 yards to go and we raced through the packed streets towards the finish before agreeing to finish together, to avoid sending Yaks, artisans and their stalls flying. I could hardly walk, and appreciated the hearty back slaps from our hosts. I'd apparently finished 16th, with Nepali athletes filling the first eight places, and 15 of the top 20. It was an education and a pleasure running in their world.

Athletes from near and far appeared to participate in a ministry of funny walks competition the following day. Not even the Nepalese athletes could walk sensibly. Each competitor had used every ounce of energy and strained every sinew to complete the marathon, and the biggest cheer had been reserved for the last competitor to finish.

After that experience I took a bigger interest in tales of races in extreme locations, and plotted my next outing. I also enjoy mountaineering and thought seriously about climbing Mt Everest, as several Everest Marathon runners had. Was it worth a hazardous trip into the death zone just to glimpse the world from the heavens? The question of why man will risk all to push boundaries intrigued me. George Leigh Mallory and Andrew Irvine's summit attempt on Everest appears to have been spurred on by what proved a fatal attraction to this mountain. Everest seemed to be neither the most difficult, nor the most aesthetic mountain in the world, although it is the highest. I wasn't interested in the most difficult, but pictures of Dhaulagiri and Manaslu were almost irresistible. I still haven't decided whether the considerable danger associated with a climb of these Himalayan giants would be excessively foolhardy. Unfortunately a plunge when climbing in New Zealand resulting in a few injuries has increased the reality of the perils of these ventures, and since that point I've preferred running, keeping my urges to climb big mountains well subdued.

The Sierra Nevada lacks the height of the Himalaya, but certainly dominate the skyline, and forced me into silence. Jennie and I share many things, including our profession, a love of mountains and ginger hair. High ground offers perspective, and I only had 200 miles before the ferry to Africa, and 30 miles into the Cordoba valley. All troubles seemed a distant memory as gravity aided my 800 metre descent into the valley where fabulous waterfalls accompanied each hair-pin bend in the road, and farmers regularly offered me oranges as they drove past, further conveying the impression of a hilly Elysian Fields.

Alas, Day 58's downhill spelt an uphill 36 miles for day 59, but distance didn't seem a problem as I jogged along warmed by the sun, enjoying the interesting terrain. I plodded along merrily, attempting to consider the potential route to the ferry as I went, and looked forward to company the next day.

Paul Bateson of Team Axarsport had offered useful advice regarding a route in Spain, as well as other local factors and I was glad that he, and another friend Keem, would join me on Day 60. Paul explained a lot of local history, and we chatted about Morocco as Keem had spent the previous week racing in the Sahara. Keem reckoned I'd love the mountains, and said I'd get plenty of company from the local kids. Finding a direct minor road was impossible and on this occasion we took the hit of running on a main road. The route was intersected by picture postcard villages, amply supplied with bakeries and cake shops which proved adequate compensation. At one point I was joined by a parapenter, who swooped and hovered above me for a couple of minutes.

Jennie and I were to be married in less than six weeks, and arrangements were ongoing. The three weeks with Jennie had given me some insight into the enormous efforts she had been putting into this, and my meagre efforts paled in comparison. I hadn't even sorted the honeymoon yet. We used her last two days in Spain to crystallise plans. Dom and Carrie from the BBC/ Triple Echo team had joined us just in time for three hours of completely torrential rain. When it rained in Spain it was drenching, and this was the hardest it had rained since Pamplona. Within ten seconds of stepping out of the van I was soaked through and at times cars aquaplaned, slithering across the road. The power of this monsoon left impressions on my skin and I jumped into the van until the rain lessened a bit. The guys had brought all sorts of ingenious contraptions with them, including a head-cam attached to a cycle helmet, which attracted some strange looks, and a camera strapped to a ski pole, which Dom would hold in front of my face as we ran together.

Day 62 was Jennie's last, and in the afternoon the sun shone on us as we clambered up to Canete Real. From here we glimpsed the Mediterranean Sea shimmering in the distance . We had to negotiate a sharp descent into the valley and when the road hair-pinned sufficiently, it was frequently possible to overtake trucks. This pleased me no end. Mum and Dad were coming out for what they hoped would be some winter sun, and Jennie would be at our friend's wedding the next day, which sadly I would miss. It was an emotional farewell, and so much would happen before I saw Jennie on my return to Scotland. However, I was also more than excited by the prospect of the wedding that I would be returning home for.

Basking in the sun

The dramatic escarpments of Ronda were to prove a gorgeous introduction to Spain for Mum and Dad. This birthplace of modern bull fighting, with its fairy tale style bridge, has inspired Orson Welles and Ernest Hemmingway and it was certainly good enough for the senior Murrays. The natural aesthetics of the surrounding area lends itself to cycling, and I was temporarily joined by a group of Spanish youngsters who chatted in English to save me further linguistic embarrassment. Birds sang and the sun shone approaching Ronda, as we gazed down on the escarpments that had repelled the Crusaders. Passing Ernest Hemmingway's former house, I stood and chatted to Dad on the bridge, peering 120 metres down into the canyon below. It was Mum's birthday, a date she shares with Elvis Presley, and Ronda seemed an appropriate place for celebration as we picnicked just outside the town. Perhaps I had over-indulged, as my lunch reappeared as soon as I hit the uphill, causing the friendly local constabulary to pull over and ask me to vomit further from the road if I would be so kind. This pair, one of which was a double for Mahoney from Police Academy, kept a close eye on me for several hundred metres as I sloped off at a snail's pace on the Algeciras road. The switchbacks that descended from the pass were magnificent, with distant peaks sparkling in the distance. A good number of memorable family photographs were taken at numerous viewpoints along the way.

Mum's birthday meal was pizza, and we ate it while watching a thunderstorm roll in at Benadalid. Rain thrashed around us, causing a brief powercut, as I considered my course of action. Tomorrow would be amazing. Almost certainly we'd see Africa, and as we were at 800 metres there would have to be ample downhill. However it was over 45 miles to the port of Algeciras, and if I wanted to visit Gibraltar, with the rock and its fascinating history, I would have to run along a motorway all the way to the airport. I never felt especially safe running on motorways although I did fancy seeing Gibraltar. I left the decision for the morning.

I'd already run two kilometres when I saw an Algeciras 78km sign. Was it worth doing the distance and making the crossing tonight? It was an attractive option, as I feared that the crossing, and Moroccan Customs, could be time-consuming, and crossing during the day could require me to run in the dark when I arrived. Days were still very short. This didn't sound ideal but neither did missing Gibraltar.

Dad, sporting his Active Nation shirt came running with me. My parents had taken me to live in Africa at the age of two, and brought me up while working in a mission hospital for six years. I couldn't have asked for a happier childhood. I was truly privileged to grow up in this way, and was proud that two of my greatest role models and inspirations would join me as Africa drew us towards her.

I got speaking to Chris, a triathlete from Gibraltar who was up training in the mountains. He explained the history of the Rock and its inhabitants and it sounded splendid but a friend scathingly suggested, "it's terrible, like Britain but with monkeys." I thought that sounded pretty good too. After much self – examination and family debate, I ran to the port arriving as the sun set on Africa, the Rif Mountains rising inexorably from the sea. I'd completed my European leg, running 261 miles that week and 2130.1 miles in total. I had now run across four countries, with only Morocco to go. My route showed me running through cities, mountains and even ski resorts before I reached the desert. My mind was racing as I failed to articulate my thoughts coherently to Carrie. All I could think about was Morocco and the finish.

CHAPTER 16

Algeciras to Er-Rachidia and the Scottish Islands Peaks Race

"Morocco's sights, smells, and sounds overload the senses."

My Lonely Planet guide assured me; "Morocco's sights, smells, and sounds overload the senses." A musty smell of too many people was the most prominent sensory stimuli as the boat pulled out from Algeciras. The rock of Gibraltar loomed large, as did Jebel Musa, guarding the Spanish enclave of Ceuta several miles distant on the Moroccan coastline. Joe Symonds and I had run the Scottish Islands Peaks Race the previous year. Teams of five sail from island to island and deposit two runners, who ascend the available peaks and run back to the boat before moving onto the next island. The mountains of Spain and Morocco, and the voyage between them, lost me in a daze recalling this race. The course takes in Oban then the islands of Mull, Jura, and Arran, before finishing in Troon. I am not in Joe's class but often go running in the hills with him. Whenever Joe and I go running I'm always infuriated and impressed with how easy he is finding it. The difference in our ability was shown at exercise testing. VO2Max looks at the body's ability to transport and utilise oxygen, and is a frequently used as a measure of the fitness of endurance athletes. My VO2Max was 69 mls/kg/minute, while Joe scored a whopping 86mls/kg/min. This compares well with world class athletes like Seb Coe, and Lance Armstrong who are reported to have achieved values of 77 mls/kg/min and 85mls/kg/min respectively although poorly with a pronghorn antelope, that when tested clocked up an unbelievable 300mls/kg/min. The highest human value recorded is 92mls/kg/minute.

First steps on the African continent. Photo – Scott Murray

Racing in Scotland. Photo – Sandbaggers

Our Islands Peaks Race team consisted of Joe and I as the runners, and Richard, Charles, and Ben as the sailors. Sunshine had greeted the start of the race in Oban, with a short run over the prominent McCaig's Folly, the highest building in the town that was intended to split the pack and avoid a log jam in the port. This being the fun run, Joe and I had dressed as pirates although the wigs and cutlasses were swiftly dispatched and my eye patch twanged off. Many teams return year after year to resume battle on the hills and high seas, and Joe chatted idly to the competition whilst I huffed and puffed around the hill. A sail over to the island of

Mull awaited us, and the apparent skill of our team in sailing was impressive. The islands on the west coast are astounding, and arriving on Mull, we figured nipping up Ben More would have us down before the dark. We were 20 minutes behind the eventual "King of the Bens" Dan Gay, and Donald Naylor, but were back on the boat as darkness fell.

The real beauty of the race is to admire the skill and stamina of the sailors who fed us like kings, and steered and sailed a course towards Jura through the foreboding Corryvreckan whirlpool. We watched dolphins and other wildlife as we went. I contributed nothing to the sailing other than a very occasional bit of rowing when the wind dropped. Arriving on Jura our sailors were knackered, having rowed the boat for many hours due to a lack of wind. We sneaked into the harbour in full stealth mode, under the cloak of darkness. The Paps of Jura dominate the island, and along with the whisky and the stock of 5500 red deer, give the island its fame. The dark adds an extra dimension to navigating over these hills with the cliffs and unstable boulder fields requiring extreme care according to the race handbook. I fell more times than I could count, and it was getting pretty light when we arrived back in Craighouse.

We glided serenely through calm waters, experiencing none of the massive swell that famously beats the Mull of Kintyre, and rounded this headland set sail for Arran. Joe sounded delighted that we were just in time for nightfall. I was glad that he'd been here before and would navigate. A trail of headtorches swarmed up Goatfell, Arran's highest peak, in a howling wind, and again I left most of the skin from my knees and elbows on the course. Even if each island was part of Scotland, arriving by boat had brought its own excitement.

On the boat to Africa, this excitement was magnified and I'd have Donnie Campbell for company on some of the Moroccan peaks. At least we wouldn't be running up them in the dark. The short crossing allowed me several pasta courses prior to disembarking in Ceuta, a Spanish colony on the African continent.

I had almost exactly 500 miles to go until I finished adjacent to the Algerian border, and the serenity of Ceuta was shattered as the border post to Morocco proper approached.

I was roasting, running in tracksuit bottoms in this Islamic country, and spotted what could easily have been a cup final crowd milling down a wide avenue. I crossed with Carrie and several cameras, and following a friendly but comprehensive interrogation from the police and customs officials we entered the grim, heavily barricaded no man's land. Immersion in Morocco was instant, with street hustlers and beggars making the world appear smaller. There can be few places in the world that offers such cultural contrast within a few hundred yards, with the elegantly European Ceuta becoming Africa in such a short distance. The volume of litter on the Moroccan side of the border had the seagulls in a frenzy, as moneychangers and touts offered a range of services. There were two possible routes, one inland and one along the coast. Having barely seen the sea since I started, and appreciating the cool breeze, I needed no persuading to follow the coast. I was soon relieved to see others out jogging, and in shorts. I needed no second invitation to replace my tracksuit bottoms with shorts and immediately had company with several Moroccan lads energetically taking up the baton from others who dropped away, usually after a kilometre or so.

Morocco has produced prodigious amounts of top class middle and long distance athletes, from Hicham El-Guerrrouj, to the legendary Ahansal brothers, kings of the Marathon des Sables, the world's most famous desert race. This association, and the sight of a camel, spurred me on despite the fatigue stemming from a poor night's sleep. Cantering through M'diq, observing the markets, and the overall busyness of my surroundings, I felt like I'd been hit by a baseball bat. In fact I had run headfirst into a road sign, much to the amusement of a few young girls who were trying extremely hard not to laugh. Blessed with a nose that has variously seen me nicknamed 'concord' and 'beaky,' I was moderately surprised to see the sign intact. Lesson learned, and with my eyes carefully watching the road in front of me I made my way around the city of Tetouan, at the base of the Rif Mountains.

Shops selling anything from wigs, dentures, car spares and fish abounded, but it was McDonald's I was most grateful as a welcome refuge for a runner desperately needing the toilet. A gentle climb along a narrow road featuring trucks with impossibly wide loads rounded off a shorter day of 34 miles, necessitated by a late start due to the border queues.

Tangier – the gateway to Morocco. Photo – Donnie Campbell

Tetouan's centre was a menace to navigate. Engrossing, lively, and tiring, the sheer weight of the crowds made food finding a three person job. Hunks of fresh fish, along with fresh vegetables and dessert came in at about £1.50, and a squirrel sized bag of nuts less than 50p. The smells emanating from the restaurant were a feast for the nose, and I soon discovered a new favourite, mint tea, which rounded off a cracking dinner. Hotel prices were similarly modest, and came with a terrific breakfast of mint tea, Moroccan bread, and eggs.

Comparing headwear in Morocco. Photo – Toby Wells

The sun rose over the Rif Mountains raising the temperature by ten degrees instantly, as kids pointed and then returned to their football. I considered joining them before realising that they were all far better than me, and jogged on to the nearest petrol station to join Mum in the hunt for reliable maps. We had three touring scale 1:100000 maps, all of which bore little resemblance to the others. The towns were the same, but with different spellings. Road junctions and rivers often varied. Little information was available concerning the quality of road surfacing on the minor roads, and indeed it was highly variable on the N13, considered a main transport artery but in reality no whopper by European standards.

This area is one of the largest hashish production areas in the world, and only modest effort is made to hide this fact. Being asked if I were interested in buying any by most males over the age of 14 in the Rif Valley evidenced this.

Chefchaouen perched majestically below Jebel El-Kelaa. It had been a long slog up into the valley, and I spent an hour watching the light shift over towering peaks, while getting some food on board. A meandering path along the river led to the Chefchaouen turnoff, and I ran past before we drove up to spend the late afternoon drinking Coke on the terrace, watching the mayhem of the souks below, and the infinitely more peaceful mountains in the distance. The climb had been less exhausting than I feared and I was heartened that another £1300 had been raised for the Yamaa Trust today by Vivergo Fuels auctioning off a Cristiano Ronaldo shirt, amongst other things. Some of the kids playing football in Chefchaouen were quite good, I'm sure Ronaldo would have approved.

Where Chefchaouen is universally acclaimed by the guidebooks, Ouezzane is less lauded. Over 37 miles had carried me through deep valleys and past several waterfalls and into a town described by Lonely Planet as "sprawling, scruffy and industrial," and by another guidebook as a place you would consider staying "only if your car suffers a mechanical catastrophe." Monaco it was not, but friends Mike and Julie, who I had stayed with near Inverness had come over to see Morocco and in Julie's case come for a run. We ate an excellent dinner served by a man whose looks closely resembled a Moroccan Joe Mangel. Mike reviewed my Achilles tendons and pronounced them to be "half the size of last time I saw them." They also described their less than triumphal entry to Morocco, the key snapping in the ignition of their hire car having cost them an extra day on the road. It meant a lot having friends and family travelling so far to be a part of the run, and Julie kept the pace lively in the early morning cool while Mum, Dad and Mike slurped the ubiquitous mint tea.

The turn-off for the road to Meknes spelled the end of the quiet roads. Overloaded trucks thundered past, distributing part of whatever they carried all over the road. Moroccan drivers were clearly used to pedestrians and animals in all forms being on the verge, and dodging in and out of the donkeys and bikes was turning into an art form.

At one point I was actually overtaken by a donkey. Curious to assess this beast's top speed, I chased it as it disappeared into the distance. Suitably impressed I googled 'donkey top speed' that night and was interested that estimates varied between 15 and 45 miles per hour. Other donkey trivia from berro.com includes the fact that more people are killed by donkeys than aeroplane crashes annually, and that a donkey will not sink in quicksand, while a mule will. Berro.com also disclosed that if angered, a horned toad will squirt blood from its eye. Armed with these facts, I slept quite well.

Moulay Idriss hides between two hills and is famed as the holiest city in Morocco. It sounded well worth a diversion and a tree lined side road looked promising. From here I turned onto a ridge, as the road climbed away from the valley. Unseasonably, it was a stiflingly hot day with the mercury topping out at 35 degrees Celcius. Several dogs chased me up the poorly surfaced road, which ultimately rewarded me with a fabulous view into the town after a knackering climb in the heat of the day. Markets bustled and loudspeakers wailed as I ran past whitewashed buildings to rejoin the main road. The Unesco World Heritage site of Volubilis was visible from the city and looked majestic, positioned on the plain before me. It was as far south as the Roman's got in Morocco and its mosaics, and views in all directions, were worth the additional kilometres. A hotel adjacent to the site had hot running water and decent food, and given the heat that day I was desperate for a shower.

Day 69 began hot and stayed hot. Having descended from the Moulay Idriss hills, it was a 1000 metre ascent to finish 36 miles later on the Azrou road. Meknes lay 33km into the route, although the suburbs and pollution of Morocco's sixth biggest city sprawled out in all directions. The highway led me through the city, with its narrow streets jammed with every kind of vehicle. By any standards the air quality was appalling, without doubt the worst I have ever encountered apart from Lima in Peru. Nothing was visible beyond the city due to a dense smog, and I was pleased to emerge spluttering on the other side, with the imposing Middle Atlas ahead. Beyond Meknes agriculture took over, with olives, pomegranates, oranges and other fresh produce sold for buttons on the side of the road.

Running beneath a blue African sky. Photo – Toby Wells

It was hot enough to require 9.5 litres of fluid that day, and from past experience I realised I'd need to replace the sodium lost by sweating and put electrolytes in every milkshake, water or coke I drunk. The hill was leniently gradual, and once up beyond El Hajeb the scenery just got better and better.

The day I ran through Meknes and up into the Middle Atlas was the day Mum and Dad headed home. Spending time with them in spectacular scenery reminded me of many enjoyable family holidays, and I had done little for myself that week other than run, navigate and blog. I think it gave them some satisfaction to see me through to so close to the finish. Their flight was from Spain, so we drove back towards the ferry, and took the opportunity of picking up Terry and Toby, who would now take command of the campervan, and Donnie, who was to run the last stretch with me. We slept in Tangier, and went our separate ways at an all too early hour, heading back past El Hajeb through the mist. One of the perils of driving in Morocco is that you never know what will fly into the middle of the road next. This is tricky in the mist, where donkeys, chickens and humans fly out in Kamikaze fashion, and it is no surprise that accident statistics are as they are. A guest house owner had told us the two critical requirements for a safe drive in Morocco were, "a good car horn and good luck." Fortunately the roads heading south from Meknes were quiet, essentially because they lead to the desert garrison towns, and there is only desert beyond them.

The road we ran on, the N13, travels north/south, whilst the Middle and High Atlas are predominantly east/ west making for an undulating, but magnificent journey. With quieter roads the amount of company from local kids also lessened, but I was pleased to have some regular company in Donnie. Donnie and I had met while competing in The Scottish Ultra, (another superb and wild race) and had often met for long runs since. A former marine commando, he was familiar with the desert and rugged terrain and he quickly updated me on all matters football, including my team Aberdeen's currently poor position. He immediately felt the difference the altitude made to his breathing and we talked considerably more on the downhills than the uphills. Terry and Toby picked a couple of magnificent spots for food stops, beside bubbling streams, and later next to a ski resort, which

204km from mayhem. Photo – Toby Wells

was pleasantly cool at an altitude of 2000 metres. We had passed Azrou, a busy Berber town, missing the famous market by a day. The slog up from the valley was compensated by the cool of a cedar and pine forest, complete with its most famed residents, the Barbary apes. This was the first location since Spain that I had seen people walking for pleasure rather than to do their daily business, and they would often encourage us with a clap or similar as we jogged past. It was also the first snow we had seen since Spain, although I declined a snow bath. The best scientific evidence suggests alternating between hot and cold baths is better than ice baths alone (which there is little good evidence for), but the showers in a rustic guest house in Timhadite offered no prospect of anything warm other than the obligatory and excellent tajine and cous cous to eat.

My taste buds had thanked me for visiting Morocco. The produce was always fresh and the local breads, tajines (a kind of stew), and dates were particular favourites. I was less sure about the similarly ubiquitous sheep head soup, often served at a stall next to the snails. Terry travels the world as an entertainer, and regaled us with stories of culinary experiences that you certainly wouldn't experience in Edinburgh. We all looked forward to the next few days, along a series of highlights that tourists flock to Morocco to see – the mountains, the Gorge du Ziz, and the Sahara were the stuff of legend, and were a world away from Le Mans on a wet Tuesday.

With my Achilles tingling slightly we re-ascended into the Atlas towards the Col du Zad. At 2174 metres we were above most of the surrounding mountains, but popped up a couple of hills near the Col to improve the view further. A turquoise lake shimmered below snowy peaks – the extra effort was well worth it. With wet feet mostly from a bog, rather than the snow, a thousand metre descent was good reward for the morning's exertions. Toby had joined us off piste in climbing the hills, and again during the descent, and told us all about his adventures catching hot air balloons in far flung places. Meeting such a diverse range of interesting people was a true privilege throughout *Scotland2Sahara*, and I was fortunate to have some of Morocco's rich traditions explained by Tariq, who was driving and guiding the Triple Echo crew. Tariq is from Merzouga, an iconic desert outpost, and despite a lifetime there he told me me words couldn't do it justice. Despite my probable anaemia and the long uphills into the mountains, Donnie and I both felt strong, and we pushed out 38 miles to Zeida relatively easily. If we did 34.5 miles a day, we'd be finished in a week, and we began to plan accordingly.

There is a flattish plain between the Middle and High Atlas mountains, and we enjoyed this on day 72. A single week seemed a trifling distance in the grand scheme of things, and having company while running, and the grandeur of our surrounds made it feel like a holiday. That is not to say that I wasn't aching all over at the end of a day, but psychologically knowing that the end was in sight, and that the weather forecast was favourable and that snow would not stop us crossing the High Atlas had allayed any anxieties I had. I also knew we'd be finishing about a week early, removing the need to run unsupported for this

The Col Du Zad in the Middle Atlas. Photo – Toby Wells

period of time. Midelt lies at the foot of the High Atlas. Jebel Ayashi, a 45km ridge of rock rises imposingly west of Midelt, and Donnie and I considered adding a side trip up its 3750 metre peak. The underfoot conditions when taking on considerably smaller mountains in the Col du Zad dissuaded us from this, and the day finished having hairpinned past Midelt into the High Atlas. In keeping with the holiday spirit we decided to stay in a nice hotel, as Tariq said prices would be low in winter here. £20 per person got us dinner bed and breakfast, hot water and internet, and all in a four-star hotel. I slept like a baby.

Emerging from a tunnel in the Atlas Mountains

Donnie was carrying injuries of his own, including an Achilles tendon injury reminiscent of mine earlier in the journey. The joy of waking up in a new place, and running somewhere beautiful, was the initial draw of an undertaking such as this for me, but Donnie's Achilles' problem was dulling this somewhat for him. We tried heel raises, running on the verge, ice and painkillers and eventually the discomfort stabilised.

The Middle Atlas hills were usually green and rolling, while the High Atlas mountains were jagged, barren and other worldly. It looked as though it hadn't rained in the valley for months, and even the summits had less snow than the Middle Atlas despite being higher. There was something of the Wild West about each settlement, although mint tea (called Berber whisky by the locals) replaced anything stronger. Eventually the sides of our valley narrowed, and the road led us claustrophobically into a gorge. The valley came to life as a river darted between rocks, bubbling downwards towards the village of Rich. Ridges appeared to form an impenetrable barrier blocking any escape south. The Atlas Mountain's predominantly East-West orientation meant that sneaking through a valley wasn't an option. Up and over had been the only choice available. I discovered the combination of coke and numerous yoghurts to be a poor one, amusing Donnie no end as I endured an unpleasant 20 minutes vomiting before retreating to the van for some medication.

Day 74 signalled an escape from the Atlas, and the start of the desert. I'd seen pictures of the French built Tunnel du Legionnaire but I'd been unable to find out much about it. Bad experiences of diverting over tunnels in Spain had led me to be suspicious of what the pictures showed to be a dark tunnel, with steep rock walls on each side. While very pretty, I was almost disappointed by the lack of challenge, as it proved to be short and perfectly safe to run through. We had considered all manner of James Bond style methods to surmount this obstacle, and laughed as we strolled though. We had entered the Gorge du Ziz, with palm fringed villages hugging the walls of the gorge, keeping us cool in the morning shadows. Beyond the gorge, barren hills stretched towards Er-Rachidia which at 37 miles was an obvious place to stop. As we guzzled electrolyte laden drinks we noticed the tar on the road had melted. I'd noticed this also on the way into Meknes, but with temperatures like this and not a cloud in the sky, I felt closer to the desert. Terry and Toby would head home today (or in Terry's case he was off to work in the Amazon on a cruise) and we looked forward to sharing a mint tea prior to them leaving. Moroccan hospitality is legendary, and nowhere more so than the hotel in Er-Rachidia. The owners had heard about the journey and its aims, and lavished us with pastries, plump locally grown dates, and mint tea. After a satisfying but hot day on the road, it was a perfect send off for Terry and Toby and excellent refuelling for Donnie and myself.

CHAPTER 17

Er-Rachidia to Erg Chebbi and The Sahara Race

"Every morning in Africa, a gazelle wakes up, it knows it must outrun the fastest lion or it will be killed. Every morning in Africa, a lion wakes up. It knows it must run faster than the slowest gazelle, or it will starve. It doesn't matter whether you're the lion or a gazelle-when the sun comes up, you'd better be running."

CHRIS MCDOUGALL

Er-Rachidia signified the start of the desert proper. The desert is a hostile and unforgiving environment, and one that I'd visited before. Our two man quest to reach each day's end reminded me of my last visit to the Sahara. I'd competed in the Sahara Race, organised by RacingThePlanet, which is part of the Four Deserts, a series of multi-day footraces across the world's most forbidding deserts. I had spent most of the week running with Canadian Mark Tamminga. These desert races are all extremely testing six-stage, 250km runs. There is no shortage of incredible things to see in Egypt, and I went backpacking along the Nile, visiting Cairo, Luxor, and Abu Simbel in the week prior to the event. Part of the attraction of the race was finishing at the Great Pyramids, and running adjacent to the ancient Valley of the Whales, where 40 million year-old fossilised whale remains have been found.

The Sahara proper. Photo – Donnie Campbell

They're off: the 2007 Sahara Race start. Photo – RacingThePlanet Ltd

EL-RACHIDIA TO ERG CHEBBI AND THE SAHARA RACE

It was the first race I'd prepared properly for, and felt a top three place was achievable. I'd trained like crazy, had my pack down to 9.4kg, and hoped acclimatising while seeing the sights would help. The unbeatable Ahansal brothers were not competing. Mark Tamminga, who had won the previous two Four Deserts events he had entered in the Atacama and Gobi deserts, was the obvious favourite.

I'd researched nutrition and acclimatisation strategy, and would carry extra food for the first day to try and get a flyer. Using the advantage of having been in Egypt for a week, I'd probably be better acclimatised than some. After 5kms I found myself in the leading pack, with everyone complaining of the heat. I felt relatively fine and deliberately stepped up the pace to beyond my own comfort zone figuring my pre-acclimatisation would be most beneficial on day one. As a complete unknown I received some funny looks as I accelerated, and bizarrely the only man to stick with me was a fellow Scot, Duncan Reid. These races attract an eclectic mix of nationalities, with about 40 nationalities represented at this race. We were literally Scot free, although the heat eventually got to Duncan, who needed an intravenous drip at the second checkpoint. The heat cranked up as midday hit, forcing me to slow down. I've always been comfortable in the extreme heat, which was certainly an advantage in this race. I figured that the hotter it became the harder everyone else would find it, especially Mark who is Canadian. I hit the finish 25 minutes ahead to claim the leader's yellow jersey.

Watching someone who knows what they are doing is always a learning experience and a privilege. I ran the following day with Mark and took it as a learning exercise, having been told his gear and knowhow were flawless for multi-stage racing. Everything was precise, with his checkpoint stops literally taking seconds. I conversely still poured potions into bottles, sorted my feet, and then spent the next few kilometres trying to catch him. Even several days later, he'd still take 30 seconds off me at checkpoints. This second day we got chatting. We're completely different people, but were running for the same reason. It was our form of tourism, and we shared a bond. Mark and his wife Joany "endured and enjoyed" these races for years and derived pleasure from the experience of seeing the world in a way that money couldn't buy.

Scot free. Leading the way with Duncan Reid. Photo – RacingThePlanet Ltd

He accelerated several times on Day Two, choosing deep sand, hills or checkpoints to do so and I was just content to run the last 5kms together once I'd caught him.

We had a similar pace, and were happy in each other's company. I knew my legs were solid over a 40km distance, and the heat didn't perturb me. The carbohydrate diet I was on was similar to all the other leaders, no matter where they were from, and as ever, everyone swapped stories and recommendations as we raced. I loved the dunes, as they were most similar to the hills I'd trained on. There was an extended dune section on Day Three, and I escaped at the front again, cheered home very sportingly by Mark's wife Joany, who was injured. The international flavour was exemplified by the flags at the campsites, although communicating with some of the South Korean and Taiwanese lads was via the international language of charades.

The multi-day events form a Tour de France type set up, with a stage each day, followed by unwinding in the evenings. The temperature had not really exceeded 45 Celcius, which is friendly by Saharan standards. There is invariably one day on these races that is anticipated and almost feared, and Day Five loomed menacingly. Running with company often makes each competitor push the other to their physical and mental limits. There was a respect between all the athletes, but as I ran with Mark each day we got on very well, while fully realising we were trying to knock lumps out of each other on the course. Day Five would be 93 kms, and as it transpired mostly straight into a chunky headwind. Any headwind will slow a runner, but the sandblasting from the Sahara was doubly tortuous. Half of the field had started two hours previously, and hauling in figures bent into the wind provided targets that kept us motivated. Running in a pair shielded one runner alternately, as we inched towards the finish. It wasn't until 70kms that we caught the quickest of the early starters, and by this time I felt like I'd eaten half of the Sahara. It became dark as we reached the 85km mark and we agreed to jog in together rather than persist with attempting to break one another. The previous 15kms had been run virtually without a word being said, with both of us admitting at the finish we'd been holding on through clenched teeth. Neither of us was prepared to budge, and I was more than happy when Mark suggested a truce. The camp lights broke a wide African sky – it could have been heaven. We were welcomed as ever by the wonderful support crew, and by some local children who were wide awake and followed us asking for pens and bon bons.

This was the first international race I'd won. More importantly, I'd run in tandem with a guy who knew exactly what works, and had unselfishly passed this on. It had shown me the power and magnificence of the Sahara, and the benefit of company. I'd had time to myself, but had better appreciated the race having someone in close proximity and being able to share experiences and witness their struggles. I certainly wasn't the quickest runner in the field (a couple of guys had 2 hrs 25 marathon times), but had withstood what the desert had thrown at us. The finish was in the most breathtaking location possible, at the Great Pyramids of Egypt. The Sphinx looked on, and each runner's jaw dropped at the sight.

The finish at the Pyramids. Photo – RacingThePlanet Ltd

Back in the Moroccan Sahara, Dave Scott and his dad Jim were due to arrive. Flying to Fez, they took an apparently bone chilling taxi ride over the Atlas in the dark and had arrived in Er-Rachidia. Ever generous, they had brought desert supplies, and we caught up with them over breakfast. Donnie, myself and Carrie had gone for a circuit of the town for sunrise and we were not disappointed. Dave and Jim must have been completely shattered, but were in fine form. Both my, and Donnie's Achilles tendons breathed a sigh of relief that we had finished with mountains and the flatter desert lands awaited. We bounded along past camels, fossil salesmen and sand dunes before stopping in awe when the land opened out below to reveal a gorge jam-packed with thousands of palm trees and people. We felt as though we had discovered a lost city and required a sit down to take it all in. This was mind blowing, my favourite sight so far, although this was being updated on an almost daily basis. This sliver of green snaked hypnotically into the distance and we were glad to follow it. Although it would have been possible to finish a day or two earlier in Merzouga, we both wanted to traverse the really big dunes near the Algerian border, and Tariq's expertise would allow us to do this. We stopped for the night in Aoufous after an easy 34 miles. I watched a belly dancing show, whereas Dave and Jim hunted for the fossils that the area is famous for. I got hold of Jennie on Skype, who couldn't believe I'd be home so early.

Dusty palm lined towns were the order of Day 76, heading yet further south to Rissani. Shoals of children, some much too fast for a body debilitated by 75 ultra marathons ran with us, and crowded round the van. Tourists became more prevalent with the high dunes a day closer. Dave and Jim said their goodbyes and headed back to Fes. We discussed the merits of dragging the sledge for the final two days. Carrying the volumes of water required in the desert on our back along with other supplies would be difficult in the sinking sand and the sledge would be a better alternative. The last two days through Merzouga, and around and into the Erg Chebbi (the biggest Moroccan dune system), would be spectacular, and the camera crew would be with us throughout. With their 4x4, they would have good access to the dunes and kindly agreed to resupply us with food and water. They had been generous with their help, warmth and support throughout, and I was grateful for this latest act of kindness. I really wanted to enjoy the last two days.

The light in the dunes was captivating as colours and sand shifted imperceptibly. It was wild and beautiful, and was what the desert looks like in central casting. My dream was being realised, and to make things even better I was told the fundraising had passed £42000. There was tranquillity in the sweeping, elegant lines of the Sahara, and satisfaction that the faith that others had shown in me had been justified. However my back had started to hurt, not the niggle that I experienced daily, but a cruel shooting pain down my leg. The dull constant pain, although sore, was no worse than my Achilles or knees had been, but the sciatica down my right leg stopped me dead on occasion. I looked at Donnie, also limping after a tough shift over the Atlas and down into the Sahara, and we got on with it, passing crumbling Kasbahs while wading through a yellow sea of sand. We were in Merzouga, the town that guards the Sahara, and the unofficial desert capital of Morocco. We'd gone cross-country but now re-entered civilisation. The desert was the star out here, tourists watched the sand open mouthed, while others were using snowboards and buggies to navigate the dunes. Camels were everywhere, unfazed by the heat or our presence.

The last day of running eventually arrived. 2630 miles down, only 29 to go. Tariq had established a route through the dunes that had us finish at a tiny village, reachable on foot, by camel, or by four- wheel drive. Good luck messages were read, breakfast eaten and sand gaiters put on. It's ironic that the most popular sand gaiters in the world are made in Paisley, and I was glad to have these symbols of Scotland in the Sahara as Donnie's gaiterless shoes filled instantly with sand. This had been a recurring theme since the sand began, and continued on this day. It is difficult to go anywhere fast in the desert, with the soft sand and heat sapping strength reserves. I had failed to stretch my back, knowing it was the last day, and I regretted this as the sciatica kicked in. It continued to get worse, giving electric shocks of pain down my leg, bringing me to the verge of tears. I cursed myself for not stretching earlier, and took as many painkillers as I was allowed. I pulled my sunglasses tighter to my face, to mask that I was close to tears. The majesty of the dunes, and the ease with which the camels moved was in sharp contrast with the Sahara's Scottish visitors. Progress on the dunes was painful and slow with each crest leading to another maze of dune. A world of sand in all directions lay below

Unforgiving dunes of the Sahara. Photo – Donnie Campbell

us from our viewpoint on the highest dunes, along with a tiny Berber village. Running down the dune to the village we laughed and smiled knowing the finish was there. The desert was everything it promised to be. Tough, sandy, hot, and no friend of back or Achilles pain, but the satisfaction in coming off the high dunes to the finish with Donnie was immense. This last day was a microcosm of the whole challenge. I never thought that the challenge would be anything other than unremittingly hard, but the highs and lows mirrored every other day.

The finish in sight. Photo – Richard Else

EL-RACHIDIA TO ERG CHEBBI AND THE SAHARA RACE

CHAPTER 18

The long road home

"Running with perseverance the race marked out for us"

HEBREWS 12:1

Drinking tea with the Berbers was a fitting way to finish. Having run nine days with Donnie, and shared the experience from planning to finish with Richard and Carrie, to finish in the heart of the Sahara among friends was perfect. We chilled for an hour listening to stories of the desert, before heading for a hotel, and writing the following entry on my blog whilst having a beer.

On day 79 I couldn't be any happier. I've just finished my run, comprising 2659 miles from John O' Groats, and finishing in the magnificent Sahara. I've had hefty pain down my right leg for the last three days. To anyone else with sciatica, views of the Sahara are pretty good painkillers. As a treat we are holed up in Maison Merzouga and having a beer. Tomorrow I'll start the long drive home, and I'm actually looking forward to seeing the scenery again, through different eyes. I've a fair respect for the High Atlas, and it will be awesome just passing through the area again. The first question I was asked by the BBC team was, "how do you feel." I definitely feel tired, and sore, but I also feel happy, and proud that I've finished the challenge. Perhaps most of all I feel grateful that I've come through it all relatively unscathed. I'm also very grateful to Jennie, and my amazing family and friends for all the support they've given me.

Arguing about football. Photo – Richard Else

I was also asked what my next challenge is, and that will be to find another beer tonight. Since the last blog, Donnie Campbell has been running with me. It's been excellent having his company and I've found it easier running with folk than solo. He's been on top form, although spent most of today emptying sand out his shoes, and I'm certain he'll be in touch with Sandbaggers for gaiters next time. It's definitely time for a shower, but thanks to all for reading and your support. Thanks also to those that have been kind enough to donate to the Yamaa Trust. It has been a huge part of the challenge, and it is fantastic for me knowing that every penny will be making a huge difference in Mongolia. Thanks also to all my fantastic sponsors Sandbaggers, Tribesport, Vivergo Fuels, UK gear, and everyone else.

I didn't need to run, and I could eat normal amounts of food. I'd spoken to Jennie
and Mum on the phone, and spent a fair bit of time doing radio and newspaper interviews as
well as taking pictures for sponsors. We were meant to start driving home but went for a walk
in the desert instead and bought souvenirs. With a heavy heart, I left the Sahara, swapping
a tee-shirt with a new friend. The drive took four days, with Donnie driving to Madrid, and then
catching a flight. My back problems had resolved and I went for a short jog near Bordeaux before
hitting the road and heading back to Edinburgh in installments. When driving home, I had the
time to reflect on the magnitude of the challenge, and the selfless efforts so many put into
Scotland2Sahara. I felt closer to Jennie and my family despite the lack of physical proximity.
It had been worth it, and I had lived and loved it. On arriving home I wrote in my blog again.

Sharing a mint tea at the finish. Photo – Carrie Hill, Triple Echo Productions

Arrived back home. Absolutely loved running out to the Sahara, but must say the drive back was a bit tedious. It was interesting virtually retracing the steps that it had taken me nearly78 days to run, and revisiting some fond memories. The terrain remained spectacular, and wild, but seemed gentler from the comfort of the campervan. Gone was the worry regarding the weather, and whether the local shops had ice, or painkillers. I had plenty of time to reflect on the run, interspersed with some fairly terrible CD's which were mostly mine.

It's easy to see the run through rose tinted spectacles and say, "that wasn't too bad", but it still strikes me how physically arduous and mentally draining I found Scotland2Sahara. It was exactly as I hoped it would be, a decent test of what my body is capable of, and I feel blessed that I chose something that although difficult, was achievable. The prevailing wind direction and the hills certainly taught me a lesson on occasion, and the one over-riding memory is that I never felt I was having to deal with these things alone, but had the support of friends, and family, and everyone else that sent me best wishes and advice. These memories will stay with me forever.

Back home I've had a shower and I now smell better than I did in the desert. The flavour saving beard has gone leaving me with a ridiculous tan line. My stats show I ran 2659 miles, and lost 0.3 kg only. I ate literally hundreds of bananas, satsumas, milkshakes, bread rolls, eating a grand total of 663 000 kilocalories. I lost 3kg running a self-sufficiency jungle race a week before starting, and I've put this back on in the last four days. An added treat for me will be to see my good friend Ian Edmond having to try to eat 20 pickled eggs in an hour. We had a sporting wager about how far I'd get, and I'm glad to avoid the fate that awaits him, and his bowels.

It's also been humbling hearing of other people's efforts and achievements. For clarity, as this is not always accurately reflected in press articles, I am pleased to have reached the Sahara to fulfil a personal ambition. It's difficult to beat seeing the Sahara sands shift during the day, and seeing the African sky at night knowing that you've tested yourself and come out the other end. The run is 25 consecutive ultra-marathons further than the Guinness world record was at the start of the challenge, but I have no desire to claim this, as I have learned about Running the Sahara, where a team consisting of Ray Zahab, Charlie Engle and Kevin Lin ran 37 miles a day for 111 days. They never claimed the record, but it would not be correct to claim a record, knowing they had exceeded it. This achievement is so colossal it has been made into a major motion picture directed by Matt Damon.

That run, and several others are just fantastic. Hugh Symond's Running High, over all 3000 feet peaks in Britain and Ireland, was a brutal accomplishment, and other great running feats include Richard Donovan's immense seven marathons in seven continents in five days. Brilliant. I'm also following Ray Zahab crossing the Atacama at present, and Sean Newell cycling between all the Commonwealth countries.

No such capers for me, as I sort out all my stuff, and leave the washing machine on non-stop. Doing some serious wedding planning this week, and there will be a preview on the Adventure Show on Tuesday, and other stuff like Reporting Scotland etc. I'll get some blood tests to confirm that I'm probably anaemic, and need to take it easy for a couple weeks but otherwise I'm tickity-boo.

On Tuesday I'll meet with Dave and Karen from the Yamaa Trust, to discuss plans for future fundraising, and projects. Any suggestions or ideas for the trust appreciated. It has astounded me to see the big-hearted response from everybody including the likes of Mark Beaumont, Ian Rankin, and Chris Cusiter."

Taking a break, but too hot for Kit Kats. Photo – Donnie Campbell

THE LONG ROAD HOME

Jennie and I were married two weeks after I got back. It was a wonderful, wonderful day and we could not have been any happier. Running was banned on the honeymoon in Sri Lanka. Other than being anaemic, which was confirmed with blood tests, I had completely recovered after a week. Two months of high dose iron tablets fixed the anaemia. I was moved by the responses of many people who have told me they have been inspired by *Scotland2Sahara* to start running, and I've even heard of running clubs being set up. So far £75000 has been donated to the Yamaa Trust through *Scotland2Sahara,* and knowing the impact this is having, we are continuing to work hard to support the people of Mongolia.

Hebrews 12:1 talks of "Running with perseverance the race marked out for us." I'll never be as quick or as strong as some, but I love new challenges and environments. During every race I've competed in, there has always been a moment that I've thought "never again," but many more thinking "what's next." One of our favourite wedding presents has been a giant atlas, and I hope to spend many happy hours leafing through it to see where that 'next' might be.

Running on the sand. Photo – Richard Else

What the Yamaa Trust means to me...

I visited Mongolia when racing the Gobi Challenge in 2009. I was immediately struck by what a wild and breathtaking place it was to visit, and what an inhospitable and difficult place it is to live.

It is the least populated country on earth. Summer temperatures reach plus 40 celcius, and Winter temperatures dip to minus 40. I could not believe the generosity of the locals, despite their profound poverty. If they could share shelter, and their food with me, surely I had to give something back.

The Yamaa Trust are making the difference day in and day out in Mongolia. Current projects include funding a deaf school, providing life changing sight restoring operations and educating and providing medical and teaching staff. I am incredibly grateful to all those that have contributed to the Yamaa Trust and have seen with my own eyes the smiles and often tears that greet the help we can provide.

Further information can be found at **www.scotland2sahara.com** and **www.yamaatrust.com**

Yamaa Trust

Going the **extra** mile for Mongolia

Like us on Facebook!

WWW.YAMAATRUST.COM

The Yamaa Trust is a registered Scottish Charity SC039727

Photo Credits

Maybe you'd like to know who kindly donated their images, or how to enter some of the races featured. Here are some further details.

Special thanks to:

"The Ultimate Marathon Man" – Triple Echo Productions, for BBC Scotland. DVD is available from Mountain Media – **www.mountain-media.co.uk**

Richard Else, Triple Echo Productions – **www.tripleecho.co.uk**

Sandbaggers, The Gobi Challenge – **www.sand-baggers.com**

Martin Like, the 6633ultra – **www.6633ultra.com**

Mike King/ Richard Donovan, North Pole Marathon – **www.npmarathon.com**

Mark Hawker, Everest Marathon – **www.everestmarathon.org.uk**

The Sahara Race, RacingThePlanet Ltd – **www.racingtheplanet.com**

Donnie Campbell – **www.skyecancercare.org**

West Highland Way Race – **www.westhighlandway.org**

Rieka Goodall, Alan Silcock, Mary Murray, Scott Murray, Susie Lind, Iain Murray, Carrie Hill and Jennie Murray.

Useful exercise/activity related sites

www.tribesports.com – Innovative social media site for sports fans!

www.sportscotland.org.uk – Scottish National Agency for Sport

www.activescotland.org.uk – Getting Scotland active